AUTISM
ENCYCLOPEDIA

The Complete Guide to Autism Spectrum Disorders

AUTISM
ENCYCLOPEDIA

EDITED BY
E. AMANDA BOUTOT, Ph.D., AND MATT TINCANI, Ph.D.

PRUFROCK PRESS INC.
WACO, TEXAS

Library of Congress Cataloging-in-Publication Data

Autism spectrum disorders handouts.
  Autism encyclopedia : the complete guide to autism spectrum disorders / edited by E. Amanda Boutot, Matt Tincani.
     p. cm.
  Originally published: Autism spectrum disorders handouts. Austin, TX : Pro-Ed, c2006.
  Includes bibliographical references and index.
  ISBN-13: 978-1-59363-360-8 (pbk.)
  ISBN-10: 1-59363-360-2 (pbk.)
  1. Autism in children—Handbooks, manuals, etc. I. Boutot, E. Amanda, 1966– II. Tincani, Matthew J. III. Title.
  RJ506.A9A87 2009
  618.92'85882--dc22
                    2008049252

Edited by Rich Restaino
Cover and Layout Design by Marjorie Parker

ISBN-13: 978-1-59363-360-8
ISBN-10: 1-59363-360-2

Printed in the United States of America.

At the time of this book's publication, all facts and figures cited are the most current available. All telephone numbers, addresses, and Web site URLs are accurate and active. All publications, organizations, Web sites, and other resources exist as described in the book, and all have been verified. The authors and Prufrock Press Inc., make no warranty or guarantee concerning the information and materials given out by organizations or content found at Web sites, and we are not responsible for any changes that occur after this book's publication. If you find an error, please contact Prufrock Press Inc.

Prufrock Press Inc.
P.O. Box 8813
Waco, TX 76714-8813
Phone: (800) 998-2208
Fax: (800) 240-0333
http://www.prufrock.com

ACKNOWLEDGMENT

The editors wish to thank Ms. Tracee Guenther for her tireless dedication to the completion of this project.

1377

124 300

CONTENTS

HOW TO
USE THIS BOOK

I N order to serve and advocate for children with autism spectrum disorders (ASD), parents, teachers, and other caretakers are faced with gathering and understanding a massive amount of information. Whereas other resources can be cumbersome and time-consuming, *Autism Encyclopedia: The Complete Guide to Autism Spectrum Disorders* offers concise, reader-friendly articles that provide answers on the most pertinent questions related to educating and parenting children with autism.

Written and edited by professional special educators and researchers, the entries explain and give practical advice on topics including the educational process; programs for young children with autism; issues in communication, behavior, and social skills; promoting functional living skills, friendships, and inclusion; and caring for adults with autism. Current research and emerging issues in treating ASD also are discussed.

Unlike some encyclopedias that use an A–Z format, the *Autism Encyclopedia* is organized by topic. Entries are grouped together under umbrella headings, such as "Overview of Autism Spectrum Disorders," "Issues in Social Skills," and "Promoting Friendships and Inclusion." Under each umbrella heading are articles that deal with a more specific topic, sometimes framed in the form of a frequently asked question, such as "How is an autism spectrum disorder diagnosed?" For those seeking quick access to specific terms, consulting the alphabetized index may prove more convenient.

Each entry contains a glossary of key terms and suggested resources for more information. Topics are cross-referenced for easy access to related articles. For example, after reading the entry on "Early Intervention Services," you may be interested in learning more about assistive technology. The *Autism Encyclopedia* makes it easy to find related topics by including page-numbered references after each entry.

The special education specialist may find it useful to use entries to help address specific concerns or questions of general education teachers or parents of children with autism spectrum disorders at IEP meetings or parent-teacher conferences. The book also may be used as part of professional development. Although useful to the professional, the entries are free of unnecessary jargon and are directed at parents seeking a more direct and active role in their child's education and development.

Perfect for parents navigating the educational system with their child, inclusion teachers, or specialists seeking a quick reference guide, the *Autism Encyclopedia* will empower all stakeholders with the information and best practices they need to help ensure success for children with ASD.

DESCRIPTION OF CONTENTS

Entries in this book are organized into 10 major topics:

- Introduction: Emerging Issues in Causes, Assessment, and Intervention provides an overview of the most up-to-date research on the major emerging issues related to the causes and assessment of autism spectrum disorders, as well as intervention techniques.

- Section 1: Overview of Autism Spectrum Disorders provides a general description of autism spectrum disorders and their diagnosis.
- Section 2: The Educational Process explains the U.S. special education system and how parents can best plan their child's education.
- Section 3: Programs for Young Children With Autism offers an overview of the different services available for young children with autism.
- Section 4: Issues in Communication highlights the different styles of communication that may be used with a child with an ASD.
- Section 5: Issues in Behavior describes variations in the stimulation of positive behaviors for a child with an ASD.
- Section 6: Issues in Social Skills describes three ways to teach social skills to a child with autism.
- Section 7: Functional Living Skills covers several strategies for assisting a child with autism in mastering daily living skills.
- Section 8: Promoting Friendships and Inclusion offers parents information on the practice of inclusion and how it will affect their child with autism.
- Section 9: Transition describes the tools necessary for a successful transition from the education system to the adult world.

INTRODUCTION: EMERGING ISSUES IN CAUSES, ASSESSMENT, AND INTERVENTION

Matt Tincani and Stacie Groeling

THE *Autism Encyclopedia* covers a variety of topics in the field of autism spectrum disorders (ASD). Our intent was to create an accessible, yet comprehensive guide for parents and professionals who wish to learn more about ASD. Within the pages of the *Autism Encyclopedia*, readers will discover a variety of topics, including programs for early intervention, techniques to promote communication and social skills, and strategies to reduce challenging behavior.

There has been much recent coverage of ASD within the media. Although the exact reasons why children develop ASD are still not well understood, researchers are working hard to identify the genetic, behavioral, and environmental risk factors underlying these conditions. At the same time, rapid strides are being made in the science of early detection and intervention. For example, a substantial body of research now suggests that young children with autism who are exposed to early, intensive interventions based in *applied behavior analysis* (ABA; see Entry 3.5) make a great deal of educational progress compared to those who are not. Teaching techniques derived from ABA—such as prompting, shaping, fading, and use of positive reinforcement—are described throughout this book. More than ever, children with ASD have the opportunity to learn new skills through the systematic applications of ABA and other research-based intervention techniques.

There have been many new advances in the field of ASD, and many more are on the horizon. What follows is a brief summary of the latest developments related to causes, assessment, and effective intervention.

WHAT CAUSES AUTISM SPECTRUM DISORDER?

The short answer to the question is "We don't know yet." Although researchers are not sure about the exact reasons why children develop an ASD, all agree that there is a strong genetic basis. The evidence for a genetic component comes from studies showing that if one identical twin is diagnosed with autism, the other is at a high risk of developing an ASD as well (Dawson, 2008). It is unlikely that a single gene causes ASD. Rather, a complex array of genes may combine with unknown environmental factors and impaired early social experiences to produce ASD in certain children. Because the exact causes are unknown, there is no medical test to diagnose an ASD. Still, advancements in research are occurring continuously, offering hope that scientists will be able to pinpoint early risk factors and identify and diagnose autism earlier, so that treatment can be as soon as possible.

Recently, a great deal of media attention has focused on the role of vaccines in the development of ASD, specifically, the measles-mumps-rubella (MMR) vaccine. There is little credible scientific evidence to suggest that the MMR vaccine causes autism;

to the contrary, many well-conducted studies strongly suggest no causal relationship between vaccines and autism (Offit, 2008). Unfortunately, some parents have chosen not to have their children vaccinated due to worries about them acquiring ASD. Consequently, dangerous childhood diseases that were eradicated through the widespread use of vaccines, such as measles, are now occurring more commonly.

ASSESSMENT OF AUTISM SPECTRUM DISORDER

Significant advancements in research have lead to the development of assessments that can reliably detect ASD in young children (Ozonoff, Goodlin-Jones, & Solomon, 2005). Early detection is critical because it enables children to receive early intervention. The Autism Diagnostic Observation Schedule (ADOS) is a direct observation tool that allows clinicians to identify ASD in children as young as 2 years old (Lord, Rutter, DiLavore, & Risi, 2002). The ADOS involves the administration of modules that create opportunities for social interaction and communication. Joint attention, which involves drawing another person's attention to an object, is an example of social interaction that is frequently impaired in children with ASD (Clifford & Dissanayake, 2008). The ADOS assesses for deficiencies in joint attention, as well as other communication and social skills. The ADOS often is administered in tandem with the Autism Diagnostic Interview–Revised (ADI-R; Rutter, LeCouteur, & Lord, 2003), a comprehensive parent interview that probes for symptoms of autism. Similar to the ADOS, the ADI-R can be used to assess ASD in children as young as 18 months old.

Unfortunately, many parents are not aware of the early signs of ASD. Consequently, ASD often is not diagnosed until two or more years after the initial signs appear (Filipek et al., 2000). In response, several major medical organizations, including the American Academy of Pediatrics, have recently developed recommendations for the screening of ASD in young children (Johnson & Myers, 2007). These guidelines instruct pediatricians to administer screenings for ASD and other developmental problems during routine well-child checkups. The Modified Checklist for Autism in Toddlers (M-CHAT; Robins, Fein, & Barton, 1999) is a 23-item screening tool to assess the risk of ASD in toddlers between 16 and 30 months of age. Children who show signs of ASD or other developmental disorders with the M-CHAT can be referred for more comprehensive diagnostic evaluations. See Entry 1.3 for more information on assessments.

EFFECTIVE INTERVENTIONS FOR AUTISM SPECTRUM DISORDER

After the diagnosis has been given, the parent of the child with ASD must seek out intervention. Many parents' first stop on the research trail is the Internet. Unfortunately, there are myriad unproven, alternative treatment packages touted to "cure" and "recover" the child with ASD advertised on the Web. A better starting point for the parent is to contact a nonprofit agency that specializes in ASD to learn more about research-based strategies and available resources. For example, Autism Speaks (http://www.autismspeaks.org) is a national organization that supports research and provides information to families of children with ASD. The Autism Society of America (http://www.autism-society.org) is another national organization that provides information and resources to families. Parents also should contact their state's departments of health and education to learn about regional and local resources. These organizations offer accurate and reliable information on local service providers, other available resources, and referrals for intervention.

There currently is no cure for autism; however, there are strategies available to help the child with ASD to make substantial communicative, social, behavioral, and educational progress. The evidence-based practice (i.e., services that have been proven in research to be effective in the treatment of autism) with the most scientific support is ABA, a scientific discipline devoted to the understanding and improvement of human behavior (Cooper, Heron, & Heward, 2007).

The following sections address commonly asked questions related to ABA and service delivery. Although the information provided is meant to inform the reader, this is not an exhaustive list of suggestions and recommendations.

WHAT IS THE DIFFERENCE BETWEEN ABA AND DISCRETE TRIAL INSTRUCTION (DTI)?

Think of ABA as an umbrella term that encompasses the principles of behavior (e.g., reinforcement, extinction, punishment; Catania, 2007; Cooper et al., 2007). Under these principles lie behavioral techniques (e.g., shaping, differential reinforcement, chaining, prompting, error correction). Approaches such as DTI, incidental teaching, and social skills instruction use behavioral principles and techniques. Therefore, DTI is an approach of ABA. So, if your child is receiving DTI, then he or she is receiving ABA.

The flowchart in Figure 1 illustrates the principles, techniques, and approaches of ABA.

```
┌─────────────────────────────────────────────────────────┐
│  ┌───────────────────────────────────────────────────┐  │
│  │              Applied Behavior Analysis             │  │
│  └───────────────────────────────────────────────────┘  │
│                          ↓                                │
│  ┌───────────────────────────────────────────────────┐  │
│  │  Principles: Reinforcement, Extinction, Punishment,│  │
│  │           Generalization, Stimulus Control         │  │
│  └───────────────────────────────────────────────────┘  │
│                          ↓                                │
│  ┌───────────────────────────────────────────────────┐  │
│  │ Techniques: Shaping, Differential Reinforcement,   │  │
│  │        Chaining, Prompting, Error Correction       │  │
│  └───────────────────────────────────────────────────┘  │
│                          ↓                                │
│  ┌───────────────────────────────────────────────────┐  │
│  │ Approaches: Discrete Trial Instruction, Incidental │  │
│  │  Teaching, Pivotal Response Training, Functional   │  │
│  │   Communication Training, Social Skills Instruction│  │
│  └───────────────────────────────────────────────────┘  │
└─────────────────────────────────────────────────────────┘
```

FIGURE 1. Principles, techniques, and approaches of ABA.

WHAT IS THE DIFFERENCE BETWEEN THE VERBAL BEHAVIOR (VB) APPROACH AND ABA?

ABA is an umbrella term that encompasses behavioral principles and techniques in which approaches are derived. The VB approach utilizes principles (such as reinforcement and extinction) and techniques (such as shaping, prompting, and generalization) to evoke verbal behavior from your child. Verbal behavior encompasses any form of communication, including spoken language, picture-based systems, and sign language (see Entries 4.1, 4.3, and 4.4). Thus, the VB approach is not separate from ABA, but is a part of it.

DOES MY CHILD NEED 40 HOURS A WEEK OF ABA OR OTHER INTERVENTION?

It is imperative to realize that the *quality* of services is more important than the *quantity* of services. Research indicates that

25 hours per week of early intervention is intensive (Steege, Mace, Perry, & Longenecker, 2007). Some children may need additional hours to achieve maximum educational progress.

Autism task forces in some states recommend 15 hours per week of intervention encompassing (a) contact hours with professionals *and* (b) engagement hours with parents/family members (New Jersey Department of Health and Senior Services, 2004). Regardless of the number of hours of intervention per week your child receives, make sure the chosen intervention is evidence-based.

HOW DO I KNOW IF MY CHILD IS RECEIVING QUALITY INTERVENTION SERVICES?

Quality intervention services are grounded in evidence-based practices. Interventions that have been scientifically demonstrated to be effective in the treatment of ASD include functional communication training (see Section 4), discrete trial instruction (see Entry 5.9), incidental teaching (also called natural environment teaching/training; see Entry 7.5), and social skills instruction, to name a few. If there is no supporting evidence that a particular treatment is effective in treating autism, then that treatment does not have "proof" of success. Examples of treatments that are not evidence-based include (but are not limited to) facilitated communication, chelation, secretin, enzymes, supplements, gluten- and casein-free diet, sensory integration, oxygen therapy, and dolphin therapy (Offit, 2008).

WHO IS QUALIFIED TO DELIVER ABA?

A professional is qualified to deliver ABA services if he or she has completed coursework and field experience under the supervision of a competent behavior analyst. The Behavior Analyst

Certification Board (http://www.bacb.com) is a national organization that gives credentials to practicing behavior analysts. The Board Certified Behavior Analyst (BCBA) credential is available to behavior analysts with master and doctoral degrees who supervise ABA programs, while the Board Certified Associate Behavior Analyst (BCABA) credential is available to practitioners with bachelor degrees who work under the supervision of BCBAs. The Association for Behavior Analysis International (http://www.abainternational.org), a professional and scholarly organization dedicated to the advancement of behavior analysis, accredits graduate training programs in behavior analysis.

Although the number of BCBAs and BCABAs continues to grow, many children with ASD receive intervention from individuals who do not hold board certification. These may include instructional aides implementing school-based ABA programs, college students implementing home-based ABA programs, classroom teachers, related service providers such as speech or occupational therapists, and even parents. A variety of stakeholders can enhance the effectiveness of ABA programs under the supervision of a competent BACB-credentialed professional.

SUMMARY

Although we still have much to learn about the causes of, assessment of, and treatment for ASD, more resources than ever are available to support early detection and effective intervention for persons with ASD. We hope you enjoy reading the *Autism Encyclopedia* and find the information valuable in your quest to learn more about ASD.

REFERENCES

Catania, A. C. (2007). *Learning* (4th ed.). New York: Sloan.

Clifford, S. M., & Dissanayake, C. (2008). The early development of joint attention in infants with autistic disorder using home video observations and parental interview. *Journal of Autism and Developmental Disorders, 38,* 791–805.

Cooper, J. O., Heron, T. E., & Heward, W. L. (2007). *Applied behavior analysis* (2nd ed.). Upper Saddle River, NJ: Merrill Prentice Hall.

Dawson, G. (2008). Early behavioral intervention, brain plasticity, and the prevention of autism spectrum disorder. *Development and Psychopathology, 20,* 775–803.

Filipek, P. A., Accardo, P. J., Ashwal, S., Baranek, G. T., Cook, E. H., Dawson, G., et al. (2000). Practice parameter: Screening and diagnosis of autism—Report of the Quality Standards Subcommittee of the American Academy of Neurology and the Child Neurology Society. *Neurology, 55,* 468–479.

Johnson, C. P., & Myers, S. M. (2007). Identification and evaluation of children with autism spectrum disorders. *Pediatrics, 120,* 1183–1215.

Lord, C., Rutter, M., DiLavore, P. C., & Risi, S. (2002). *The autism diagnostic observation schedule.* Los Angeles: Western Psychological Services.

New Jersey Department of Health and Senior Services. (2004). *Service guidelines for children with autism spectrum disorders.* Retrieved from http://www.state.nj.us/health/fhs/documents/autismguidelines.pdf

Offit, P. A. (2008). *Autism's false prophets: Bad science, risky medicine, and the search for a cure.* New York: Columbia University Press.

Ozonoff, S., Goodlin-Jones, B. L., & Solomon, M. (2005). Evidence-based assessment of autism spectrum disorders in children and adolescents. *Journal of Clinical Child and Adolescent Psychology, 34,* 523–540.

Robins, D., Fein, D., & Barton, M. (1999). *The modified checklist for autism in toddlers (M-CHAT).* Storrs: University of Connecticut.

Rutter, M., LeCouteur, A., & Lord, C. (2003). *ADI-R: Autism diagnostic interview—Revised.* Los Angeles: Western Psychological Services.

Steege, M. W., Mace, F. C., Perry, L., & Longenecker, H. (2007). Applied behavior analysis: Beyond discrete trial teaching. *Psychology in the Schools, 44*, 91–99.

OVERVIEW OF AUTISM SPECTRUM DISORDERS

DOES MY CHILD HAVE AN AUTISM SPECTRUM DISORDER?

E. Amanda Boutot

PARENTS often are the first persons to recognize that something is not right with their child's development and to bring it to the attention of their pediatrician or a family friend. Parents are the best judges of how their children are developing because they see them daily and have known them since birth. This entry highlights some of the characteristics of autism spectrum disorders (ASD) that appear, starting at birth, as well as early developmental delays that may be expected in a child with an ASD.

CHARACTERISTICS FROM BIRTH

In 2002, Connie Kasari and Connie Wong, researchers at UCLA, identified five early signs of autism as outlined in this entry. Although ASD typically are not diagnosed until a child is at least 3 years old, many parents begin to have concerns about their child's development by the time he or she is 18 months old. Because early intervention for children with autism is crucial to future development and in helping a child reach his or her full potential in later years, early diagnosis is critical. These five early signs are suggested as flags of concern for parents and professionals and indicate a need for further testing.

SIGN 1: DOES YOUR INFANT RESPOND WHEN A CAREGIVER CALLS HIS OR HER NAME?

Typical babies are very responsive to familiar voices and within the first few months of life will turn toward a caregiver who is calling their name. According to Kasari and Wong (2002), however, babies who are later diagnosed with an ASD turn toward the caregiver only about 20% of the time. In addition, they may ignore sounds and may be unresponsive to familiar voices while at the same time focusing on other sounds in their environment. As Kasari and Wong noted, "they may fail to respond to their parent calling their name, but immediately respond to the television being turned on" (p. 61). In these situations, many parents of children later diagnosed with an ASD initially feared their child had a hearing impairment.

SIGN 2: DOES YOUR INFANT ENGAGE IN JOINT ATTENTION?

Joint attention is seen in a young child (around age 1) who is able to join an adult or other person in looking at an object of interest. Typical infants will begin to follow a person's finger pointing or gaze very early on, and later, around age 1, they will begin to gaze at items of interest and point out items to others. Children with an ASD, by contrast, rarely follow the pointing of others, cannot shift their gaze from objects to people, and do not engage in joint attention to objects or events with others. While typical children will show favored items to their caregivers, children later diagnosed with an ASD rarely engage in this sort of "sharing."

SIGN 3: DOES YOUR INFANT IMITATE OTHERS?

"Typical infants are mimics." (Kasari & Wong, 2002, p. 61). Parents of typical babies have reported their child's ability to imitate facial expressions as early as when the child is a few days old. They have noted the ability to imitate sounds and complex hand and body movements (such as clapping) by the time the child is 8–10 months old. Children with an ASD, on the other hand, rarely imitate the expressions or actions of others.

SIGN 4: DOES YOUR INFANT RESPOND TO OTHERS EMOTIONALLY?

Typical infants smile when others smile at them and are socially responsive to those around them. For example, when a typical infant sees another child crying, he or she will show an expression of concern or sadness; older infants or young children will try in some way to comfort the unhappy person. Children later diagnosed with an ASD, however, seem unaware of the emotional states of others. They rarely smile when others smile, and they do not show concern or seek to comfort those in distress; in fact, they are more likely to ignore the person than to respond in any way.

SIGN 5: DOES YOUR INFANT PRETEND PLAY?

Toward the end of the first year, the play of infants begins to take on a pretend quality; by the second year, toddlers engage in more advanced forms of imaginative play, such as "playing house." In contrast, children with an ASD may have no interest in toys, or if they do, they play with the toy in a repetitive fashion rather than engaging in true play. For example, a child with an ASD may play with a toy truck by turning it over and spinning the wheels rather than pushing it along a path. According to Kasari and Wong (2002), pretend play is nearly absent in children with an ASD under the age of 2.

These five early signs of ASD may or may not be present in every infant who is later diagnosed with an ASD. They are a good guide, however, for parents and physicians to follow when determining whether a delay in development requires further evaluation.

DEVELOPMENTAL DELAYS IN ASD

By definition, autism spectrum disorders are developmental disabilities; therefore, it is not surprising that delays in development can be seen very early in infants and young children later diagnosed with an ASD. The obvious delays are in the areas of communication and social relations, as defined in the text revision of the *Diagnostic and Statistical Manual–Fourth Edition* (DSM-IV-TR) of the American Psychiatric Association (2000). For many toddlers and preschoolers with an ASD, other areas of delay—such as gross and fine motor development—also may be present. Each of these areas is discussed in further detail in this section.

COMMUNICATION DEVELOPMENT

Between 9 and 13 months of age, typical children achieve skills that are key to later communication. First, they begin to use signals and gestures with the intent of communicating needs and desires. Second, they begin to discover that things have names; they apply meaning to the words they hear. This is an important first step in later communication and speech development.

Many children with autism fail to develop these simple abilities and thus also fail to develop meaningful communication. Even among those children with autism who are able to make their wants and needs known to caregivers, many may not develop speech. Very young typical infants display the prespeech production known as "babbling," which is simply putting together single sounds, such as "ba," and practicing them over and over: "ba, ba, ba." Later, usually by age 1, infants begin to use one-word, sentence-like phrases called *holophrases*. As an example, a child might say "dog," which could mean, "I see the dog," "I want the dog," or "Help, the dog just licked me!" By 18 months of age, speech has progressed to sentences of two or more words in typical children. By age 2, most typical children can name all familiar objects and people around them and can put together multiple-word, meaningful sentences that include adjectives and adverbs and that vary in intonation and inflection. Children with an ASD, even when they do develop speech, may do so significantly later than typical children or may appear to progress to a certain point and then stop. It is important to remember that for all children the ability to communicate is not limited to speech alone; however, no matter the form of communication, the intent and the recognition of things as having names is crucial.

SOCIAL DEVELOPMENT

As previously mentioned, when they are just a few days old, typical infants begin to respond to others through imitation; by several months of age, they are able to respond to the emotions of others. These are crucial parts of social development because they set the stage for learning the rules of relating socially later in childhood. Because children with an ASD rarely are able to recognize such subtleties as facial expression, tone of voice, or body language, they have difficulty with social development from very early on. They also may respond differently than their typical peers to social occurrences such as reprimands or jokes.

FINE AND GROSS MOTOR DEVELOPMENT

Some parents have reported that their child with an ASD developed many skills at a slower rate than did typical children. Examples include sitting up, rolling over, crawling, walking, and climbing stairs. Although many factors may contribute to a child's delay in achieving these and other skills at the typical age—and physicians are quick to point out that all children develop at different rates—it is still clear that a child who is later diagnosed with an ASD may show signs of developmental delay in all areas. These early motor delays should therefore be watched closely.

SUMMARY

Parents must feel empowered to recognize the possibility of delays in their child's development and bring them to the attention of pediatricians and others so that appropriate early intervention can begin as soon as possible. This entry listed several developmental areas that may be delayed or lacking for children with an ASD and that are noticeable from early infancy. Such delays may exist in children who are not later diagnosed with an ASD, however, and at the present time there is no early test for ASD.

REFERENCES

American Psychiatric Association. (2000). *Diagnostic and statistical manual of mental disorders* (4th ed., Text rev.). Washington, DC: Author.

Kasari, C., & Wong, C. (2002). Five early signs of autism. *Exceptional Parent*, 32(11), 60–62.

PRINT RESOURCE

Lefrancois, G. R. (1995). *Of children*. Belmont, CA: Wadsworth.

KEY TERMS

HOLOPHRASES: Single words used as an entire phrase, for example, "doggy" to mean "I see the doggy"

JOINT ATTENTION: Gazing at a point of interest (usually an object, activity, or person) with another person such that they are "jointly" attending to the point of interest

PRETEND PLAY: Play that takes on imaginative forms (e.g., "cooking" in a pretend kitchen) or that involves playing with items as if they were something else (e.g., "flying" a brush as if it were an airplane)

SEE ALSO THESE RELATED ENTRIES:

WHAT ARE AUTISM SPECTRUM DISORDERS?

E. Amanda Boutot

CURRENT statistics suggest that as many as 1 out of 150 people have an autism spectrum disorder (ASD). This is an extraordinary number when you realize that as few as 15 years ago, it was said to be only 4 to 5 out of 10,000 (Simpson & Regan, 1988). The reason for this increase is unknown; however, more public awareness and efforts by various organizations to help with earlier and more accurate diagnosis may be contributing factors. This entry briefly describes the characteristics, causes, and treatment issues of ASD.

TYPICAL CHARACTERISTICS

Characteristics of autism range from very mild to severe. Generally speaking, a child diagnosed with Asperger's syndrome or pervasive developmental disorder–not otherwise specified (PDD-NOS) will display milder symptoms than a child with a diagnosis of autism. No two children with an ASD are alike, regardless of the specific diagnosis, and there are a range of symptoms, any of which a child may have to various degrees. For example, a child may have a diagnosis of autism but show less severe symptoms than another child with the same diagnosis or a child with another ASD. Overgeneralized, stereotyped statements such as, "All children with ASD . . ." or even "Most children with ASD . . ." are inappropriate and send a false message about the nature of these disorders. Although similar in terms of diagnostic criteria, various ASD occur in very different ways for each person. The following is a list of some typical characteristics:

- delay or lack of speech (not seen in Asperger's syndrome);
- resistance to change or changes in routine;
- insistence on similarity or repetition;
- lack of eye contact;
- sensitivity to sensory sensations such as light, sound, touch, or certain textures;
- repetitive behaviors, known as "self-stimulatory behaviors," such as rocking, hand-flapping, or spinning objects;
- lack of pretend play;
- inability to initiate or sustain a conversation;
- lack of imitation;
- aloofness;
- preference for being alone;
- echolalic speech (repeating what has been said); and
- seeming not to hear others.

Although these are only a few of the possible characteristics that a person with an ASD may have, they may occur in varying degrees of severity, and an individual with one of these disorders may display them differently from another person.

CAUSES OF ASD

At this time, there are no known causes of ASD. They are, however, generally regarded as neurological disorders that negatively affect development in at least one part of the brain. In other words, something in the brains of people with an ASD does not develop and work as it should. This could include neurotransmitters (neurons) or different regions of the brain. Whether this is due to a faulty gene, a chromosomal abnormality (such as Fragile X syndrome), or some other damage is not known at this time. Researchers are frantically searching for an exact cause of ASD, and multiple causes ultimately may be found. Although several theories as to specific causes (e.g., vitamin deficiencies, vaccines) have been studied, there seems to be no conclusive link between any one specific agent and ASD. There may even be multiple causes for an ASD in one person.

IS THERE A CURE?

Given that no known cause has been identified to this point, there is no known cure. Many treatments that may be effective in reducing or even eliminating symptoms have been proposed, but until the exact nature of the disorders is known, a cure is not possible.

PROGNOSIS

Do not be discouraged by the lack of knowledge about the causes of ASD or by the lack of a known cure. Many people with an ASD grow up to lead successful, contributing, and independent lives as adults. Early and effective intervention is key. In terms of a cure, think of an ASD as similar to the common cold: Although a cure has not been identified, treatment of the symptoms is possible.

EFFECTIVE TREATMENT

Education and effective treatment can be called the "aspirin" for ASD. Over the years, various educational treatments—some with much success and others with minimal success—have been identified. The most important goal of any educational program or treatment is to help the person with an ASD become more functionally independent. This may involve teaching her or him how to communicate with others; how to develop appropriate play, work, or social skills; or how to modify behaviors. Parents should do their homework when considering a particular treatment option for their child and also should consider many options. Other entries in this book address specific treatment options that may be available to parents.

SUMMARY

Although much about ASD remains a mystery, more informa tion is coming in daily from researchers and professionals in the field. Parents need to know that they are not alone in dealing with an ASD. Parent support groups exist in almost every major community, and services for families often are available in rural areas as well. Parents are encouraged to contact one or more of these organizations to determine the types of local support, available programs, and other important information specific to their community or area. A wealth of information is available through other resources, and families should educate themselves with as much information about ASD as possible. You are the experts on your children; the more you know, the better you can help them learn and develop.

REFERENCE

Simpson, R. L., & Regan, M. (1988). *Management of autistic behaviors.* Austin, TX: PRO-ED.

PRINT RESOURCE

American Psychiatric Association. (2000). *Diagnostic and statistical manual of mental disorders* (4th ed., Text rev.). Washington, DC: Author.

KEY TERMS

FRAGILE X SYNDROME: The most common inherited form of mental retardation; a genetic disorder caused by the body's inability to produce the protein FMRP

PERVASIVE DEVELOPMENTAL DISORDER–NOT OTHERWISE SPECIFIED (PDD-NOS): According to the text revision of the fourth edition of the *Diagnostic and Statistical Manual of Mental Disorders*, a child who has significant difficulties with social interactions, verbal and nonverbal communication, and play—difficulties are not severe enough to warrant the diagnosis of autism

SEE ALSO THESE RELATED ENTRIES:

HOW IS AN AUTISM SPECTRUM DISORDER DIAGNOSED?

E. Amanda Boutot

AUTISM spectrum disorders (ASD) are part of a group of disorders known as pervasive developmental disorders (PDDs), as defined in the text revision of the *Diagnostic and Statistical Manual of Mental Disorders* (DSM–IV–TR; American Psychiatric Association, 2000). Included in the manual are autism, Asperger's syndrome, and pervasive developmental disorder–not otherwise specified (PDD-NOS). Physicians and psychologists use the DSM–IV–TR to diagnose mental health disorders. School psychologists, educational diagnosticians, and other school personnel typically use the federal definition of autism from the Individuals with Disabilities Education Act (IDEA):

> A developmental disability significantly affecting verbal and nonverbal communication and social interaction, generally evident before age 3, that adversely affects a child's performance. Other characteristics often associated with autism are engagement in repetitive activities and stereotyped movements, resistance to environmental change or change in the daily routines, and unusual responses to sensory experiences. The term does not apply if a child's educational performance is adversely affected primarily because the child has a seri-

ous emotional disturbance. (U.S. Department of Education, 34 C.F.R. 300, § 300.7 [b][1])

The federal government makes no distinction among the types of autism spectrum disorders; thus, a student with Asperger's syndrome or PDD-NOS may qualify for special education services under the definition of autism although his or her physician has not made that specific diagnosis. This can be confusing for parents and other adults, but it is important to note that all of the disorders on the spectrum are similar in terms of their social and educational needs. As such, a label of autism often is sufficient to obtain the necessary services for an appropriate education.

ASSESSMENTS

There is no medical test for an ASD, and the decision to diagnose or label a child with one of these disorders is up to the persons in charge of assessing that child. A psychologist or physician using the DSM–IV–TR as a diagnostic tool usually will perform a battery of tests, including an IQ test, interview the family, and observe or interview the child. This often can be completed in one visit. In the case of education, parents should be involved in the assessment process and also contribute to the decision to apply the autism label. Making the decision to label a child with autism for the purposes of providing special education services may involve a variety of people employing several types of assessments. These assessments may include the following:

- an IQ test;
- developmental checklists;
- behavior checklists;
- autism-specific surveys or checklists;
- interviews with family members and other teachers;

- observations of the child;
- occupational, physical, and speech therapy assessments; and
- examination of school records—including grades and school-work, where applicable.

Although there is no one diagnostic tool for labeling or diagnosing an ASD, several checklists are available to help parents and professionals determine the likelihood that a child has the disorder.

SUMMARY

Autism spectrum disorders encompass a variety of individual characteristics that in combination lead to a diagnosis or label. The primary purpose of "labeling" a child or adult with a particular disorder is to allow the person's caregivers to obtain specific services for which the diagnosed person would not be eligible were it not for the label. In the U.S. education system, students are automatically entitled to individualized services once they are determined to have a disability, disorder, or other impairment that impacts their ability to learn. As adults, many people qualify for specialized services, such as help with employment, transportation, or living options, based on a certain diagnosis. An ASD diagnosis for a child can allow him or her to have assistance to help make learning and independence easier in the future.

REFERENCES

American Psychiatric Association. (2000). *Diagnostic and statistical manual of mental disorders* (4th ed., Text rev.). Washington, DC: Author.

U.S. Department of Education. (1997). *Nineteenth annual report to Congress on implementation of the Individuals with Disabilities Education Act.* Washington, DC: Author.

WEB RESOURCES

Autism Society of America (http://www.autism-society.org)

Autism Speaks (http://www.autismspeaks.org)

Division TEACCH (http://www.teacch.com)

Families for Early Autism Treatment (http://www.feat.org)

Lovaas Institute for Early Intervention (http://www.lovaas.com)

National Autistic Society (United Kingdom) (http://www.nas.org.uk)

National Institute of Mental Health (http://www.nimh.nih.gov/publicat/autism.cfm)

KEY TERMS

FREE APPROPRIATE PUBLIC EDUCATION (FAPE): A part of the special education law that states that schools cannot deny education to any child on the basis of his or her disability

INDIVIDUALS WITH DISABILITIES EDUCATION ACT (IDEA): Federal legislation providing free, appropriate education to all children with disabilities in public schools

SEE ALSO THESE RELATED ENTRIES:

ABOUT ASPERGER'S SYNDROME

Matt Tincani

N 1944, Viennese Psychiatrist Hans Asperger described a condition that would later be called *Asperger's syndrome* (AS). Individuals with AS encounter difficulties with social skills and are prone to restricted or unusual interests. Unlike autism, persons with AS do not have delayed spoken language, and tend to have normal or above average intelligence. AS was considered to be an obscure condition until the early 1990s when, thanks to the work of Uta Frith (1991) and others, it began to receive the attention it deserved. Today, AS, along with autism and pervasive developmental disorder–not otherwise specified (PDD-NOS), is regarded as a disorder within the autism spectrum.

CHARACTERISTICS OF AS

Children with AS develop speech and language at the same rate as children without disabilities. However, other aspects of communication are impaired. Some children with AS understand language very literally, which can make it difficult for them to understand idioms and jokes or interpret the behavior of others, including gestures. For example, a child with AS may become confused upon hearing phrases such as "He brings home the bacon" or "It's not my cup of tea." Comprehending other people's feelings or emotions can be especially challenging (Safran, 2001). For instance, a person with AS may have difficulty understanding why someone is upset with him or her, due to difficulties reading social cues that seem obvious to others. Problems with the social aspects of language render children and adolescents with AS prone to bullying, can produce high anxiety in social situations, and form barriers to friendships with typical peers (Smith Myles & Simpson, 2002).

Restricted or unusual interests also are a concern in AS. Children with AS often become fascinated with a particular topic, which dominates their conversations with others. The topic can be just about anything, such as trains, baseball, or horses. Their tendency to initiate social interactions with a favorite topic limits their ability to engage in meaningful, reciprocal social interactions. Additional characteristics of AS include (Smith Myles & Simpson, 2002):

- social stiffness and awkwardness,
- inflexibility with routines,
- concrete and literal thinking,
- good comprehension of factual material,
- poor organizational skills,
- emotional vulnerability and stress,
- sensory problems,
- clumsiness, and
- depression.

PREVALENCE AND DIAGNOSIS OF AS

The prevalence of autism spectrum disorders (ASD) currently is estimated to be about 1 in 150 people in the U.S. (See Entry 1.2). Few researchers have examined the subprevalence of AS within

ASD. Data from a limited number of studies suggests that AS occurs less frequently than autism (Fombonne, 2005). However, it is important to consider that AS may be underreported due to the high functioning nature of children with the disorder. Like autism, more boys than girls receive the AS diagnosis.

ASD, including AS, are diagnosed according to the text revision of the *Diagnostic and Statistical Manual of Mental Disorders* (DSM-IV-TR; American Psychiatric Association, 2000; see Entry 1.3). Clinicians often use instruments in the diagnosis that are specifically designed to address the characteristics of AS. For example, the Asperger's Syndrome Screening Questionnaire (ASSQ; Ehlers, Gillberg, & Wing, 1999) is a tool completed by parents or teachers to screen for AS in school-aged children.

INTERVENTIONS FOR AS: A STRENGTH-BASED PERSPECTIVE

Despite their difficulties, persons with AS have positive qualities that can be utilized to develop effective interventions. Although children with AS tend to focus their conversations on a particular topic of interest, they also tend to become experts on that topic. Many individuals with AS excel in careers that involve a highly specialized interest area. For instance, a young man who is particularly fascinated with numbers may have strong aptitude for a career in mathematics, computer science, or a related field. By engaging a student in his or her special interest area, teachers can encourage conversations, reduce anxiety, and increase academic motivation (Winter-Messiers et al., 2007). There are many tools on the market to help parents and educators capitalize on the special interest areas of children with AS. For example, the Power Card is a wallet-sized card that depicts a student's special interest and contains a script detailing how to navigate a social situation, solve a specific problem, or engage in a daily routine (Gagnon, 2001). Interventions like Social Stories (Gray & Garand, 1993; see Entry 6.1) also can be effective in teaching children and adolescents with AS the rules of appropriate interactions for specific social situations.

REFERENCES

American Psychiatric Association. (2000). *Diagnostic and statistical manual of mental disorders* (4th ed., Text rev.). Washington, DC: Author.

Ehlers, S., Gillberg, C., & Wing, L. (1999). A screening questionnaire for Asperger syndrome and other high functioning autism spectrum disorders in school age children. *Journal of Autism and Developmental Disorders, 29,* 129–141.

Frith, U. (Ed.). (1991). *Autism and Asperger syndrome.* Cambridge, UK: Cambridge University Press.

Fombonne, E. (2005). The changing epidemiology of autism. *Journal of Applied Research in Intellectual Disabilities, 18,* 281–294.

Gagnon, E. (2001). *Power cards: Using special interests to motivate children and youth with Asperger syndrome and autism.* Shawnee Mission, KS: Autism Asperger Publishing Company.

Gray, C. A., & Garand, J. D. (1993). Social stories: Improving responses of students with autism with accurate social information. *Focus on Autistic Behavior, 8,* 1–10.

Safran, S. P. (2001). Asperger syndrome: The emerging challenge to special education. *Exceptional Children, 67,* 151–160.

Smith Myles, B., & Simpson, R. (2002). Asperger syndrome: An overview of characteristics. *Focus on Autism and Other Developmental Disabilities, 17,* 132–137.

Winter-Messiers, M. A., Herr, C. M., Wood, C. E., Brooks, A. P., Gates, M. A. M., Houston, T. L., et al. (2007). How far can Brian ride the Daylight 4449 Express? A strength-based model of Asperger syndrome based on special interest areas. *Focus on Autism and Other Developmental Disabilities, 22,* 67–79.

KEY TERMS

Asperger's Syndrome Screening Questionnaire (ASSQ): A checklist completed by parents or teachers to assess for symptoms characteristic of Asperger's syndrome

Power Card: A wallet-sized card that depicts a student's special interest, and contains a script detailing how to navigate a social situation, solve a specific problem, or engage in a daily routine

SEE ALSO THESE RELATED ENTRIES:

THE
EDUCATIONAL
PROCESS

UNDERSTANDING SPECIAL EDUCATION

Susan M. Silvestri, Natalie J. Allen,
Charles L. Wood, Michelle A. Anderson,
Corinne M. Murphy, and William L. Heward

FOR most children, the general education curriculum and instruction are effective. Children who have or who are at risk for developing cognitive, physical, health, sensory, and behavioral disabilities, however, often need special education. If your child is diagnosed with an autism spectrum disorder (ASD), he or she will receive special education services. In this entry, we define the term *special education* from functional and legal standpoints; explain terms such as *IEP, related services,* and *LRE;* and provide a broad view of the evaluation and referral process used to determine the type and extent of special education services that a child will receive.

DEFINITION AND PURPOSE OF SPECIAL EDUCATION

Federal law defines special education as "specially designed instruction, at no cost to the parent, to meet the unique needs of a handicapped child" (Individuals with Disabilities Education Act Amendments, § 300.14, 1997). At the level where students with disabilities are most meaningfully and frequently involved with special education, it should be "individually planned, special-ized, intensive, goal-directed instruction" designed to prevent, eliminate, or overcome the obstacles that might keep the student from learning and from full and active participation in school and society (Heward, 2003, p. 38). Special education includes:

- *Prevention* is designed to eliminate or reduce the effects of risk factors—such as low birthweight or neglect—so that a disability never develops.
- *Remedial instruction* is aimed at eliminating or reducing the effects of an existing disability and includes teaching skills—such as self-care and vocational skills—that will help the student lead an independent life.
- *Compensatory intervention* teaches a person with a disability to use skills and devices that help him or her perform important tasks and function in spite of the disability.
- *Compensation* includes assistive technology devices such as magnifiers for individuals with vision problems.

IDEA: SPECIAL EDUCATION LAW

In 1975 the U.S. Congress passed a law with two main purposes:

1. to ensure that all children with disabilities had available to them a public education that recognized and responded to their unique needs, and
2. to protect the rights of children with disabilities and their parents in the educational process.

This law, which today is called the Individuals with Disabilities Education Act (IDEA), has been amended several times. The majority of the many resulting rules and regulations that mandate how schools design and deliver special education services have remained unchanged, however, and can be summarized under the major principles described next.

ZERO REJECT

Schools are responsible for finding, evaluating, and educating all students with disabilities. No school can tell a parent that a child is too disabled to receive or benefit from special education services. A parent who suspects that his or her child has a disability can ask the school district to do an evaluation. In addition, the "child-find system" requires each state to locate, identify, and evaluate all children up to the age of 21 years who live in that state and who have or are suspected of having a disability.

NONDISCRIMINATORY IDENTIFICATION AND EVALUATION

School districts must provide an unbiased and multifactored evaluation (MFE) at public expense. To determine a child's cognitive, behavioral, developmental, and physical skills and deficits, the district must use evaluation that includes a variety of assessment formats (e.g., formal assessments, such as achievement and language tests, and informal assessments, which include classroom observations and interviews with the child's teacher). Assessments must be conducted in the child's native language. Teachers, psychologists, and specialists, along with other involved adults, participate on the evaluation team. Parents must give their consent before any evaluations or assessments are given, and they may be able to obtain independent evaluations at public expense.

FREE APPROPRIATE PUBLIC EDUCATION

If it is determined that a child has a disability, the school district must provide a free appropriate public education (FAPE). This means that special education services are to be provided at public expense, should be designed to allow the child to benefit from these services, and must be provided according to each child's needs.

INDIVIDUALIZED EDUCATION PROGRAM (IEP)

The IEP is the centerpiece of special education. After the evaluation, IEP planning begins. In this stage, the IEP team meets to determine appropriate goals and services for the child. They use the multifactored evaluation and other relevant information to do this. Team members include the parents, a general education teacher, a special education teacher, a person who can interpret the results of the evaluation, and a school district representative, plus any other persons who have relevant knowledge or appropriate expertise. A parent representative may participate, and parents can bring an advocate. If appropriate, the child also may participate as a member of the team. The IEP is revised and updated every year, evaluations are conducted at least every 3 years, and progress on IEP goals and objectives is reviewed and communicated to parents at least as often as the school district communicates progress for children without disabilities.

The IEP must include the following components:

- a statement about the child's present level of performance, including how the child's disability affects his or her involvement in the general education curriculum;
- a statement of measurable annual goals, including short-term objectives;

- a statement of the special education and related services—and supplementary aids and services—to be provided;
- an explanation regarding how much the child will participate with nondisabled children;
- a statement about modifying how state or district assessments are given;
- the projected date for the start of services; and
- a statement as to how the child's progress will be measured and how the parents will be informed of this progress.

Any related services the child may need so he or she will benefit from special education are specified on the IEP. These services may include:
- assistive technology devices and services;
- audiology (for children with hearing impairments);
- counseling services, including rehabilitation counseling;
- early identification and assessment of disabilities in children;
- health services (by a school nurse or other qualified person);
- medical services (by a licensed physician for diagnostic or evaluation purposes);
- occupational therapy (OT);
- orientation and mobility services (for children with visual impairments);
- parent counseling and training;
- physical therapy (PT);
- psychological services;
- recreation, including therapeutic recreation;
- speech pathology and language services; and
- transportation services.

LEAST RESTRICTIVE ENVIRONMENT

IDEA mandates that students with disabilities be educated to the greatest extent possible with same-age children without disabilities. This is based on the belief that the general education classroom is the best place for a child with disabilities to receive educational services. A child with a disability should not be removed from the general education classroom unless his or her disability is so severe that he or she cannot benefit from the services. In this case, the IEP must include a statement justifying the extent to which a child will not participate with same-age nondisabled children and in the general curriculum. According to IDEA, the child must receive services in the least restrictive environment (LRE) in which an appropriate education can be provided and in which he or she can benefit from those services.

DUE PROCESS SAFEGUARDS

IDEA includes safeguards to protect the rights of parents and students with disabilities. Parents have the right to challenge or appeal any decision related to the identification, evaluation, or placement of their child. If parents disagree with any decisions, schools must provide the opportunity to resolve issues with a mediator or via a hearing. Schools must maintain confidentiality of student records, and parents have the right to review any documents related to their child's educational services.

PARENT AND STUDENT PARTICIPATION
AND SHARED DECISION MAKING

Schools must consider the parents' input and wishes and—whenever appropriate—the student's thoughts and desires in all aspects of the special education process, including selection of

IEP goals and objectives, determination of related service needs, and placement decisions.

SUMMARY

Becoming familiar with the process, goals, and requirements of special education services will enable parents to advocate more effectively for their children and to ensure that they receive an education that will meet their needs. Not only can parents participate equally in planning for the short term, they also can be better prepared to plan for the long term.

REFERENCE

Heward, W. L. (2003). *Exceptional children: An introduction to special education* (7th ed.). Upper Saddle River, NJ: Merrill/Prentice Hall.

Individuals With Disabilities Education Act Amendments §300.14 (1997).

PRINT RESOURCES

Cutler, B. C. (1993). *You, your child, and "special" education: A guide to making the system work*. Baltimore: Brookes.

Siegel, L. M. (2001). *The complete IEP guide: How to advocate for your special child* (2nd ed.). Arlington, VA: Council for Exceptional Children.

KEY TERMS

CONTINUUM OF SERVICES: Options for educating a child with disabilities in the most appropriate setting for provision of his or her IEP goals; services range from full inclusion in a general education setting, to self-contained, to hospital or residential

Due process safeguards: Rights allowing parents and families a voice in their child's education; procedures for filing a grievance when disagreements occur

Free appropriate public education (FAPE): A part of the special education law that states that schools cannot deny education to any child on the basis of his or her disability

Individuals with Disabilities Education Act (IDEA): Federal law providing for FAPE and other education service for children with disabilities

Individualized Education Program (IEP): A document detailing a child's needs and strengths, as well as what the school will be responsible for teaching during a specified amount of time

Least restrictive environment (LRE): A statement in IDEA that children with disabilities must be educated in accordance with a continuum of services

Related services: Services that support a child's education; these include speech therapy, occupational therapy, physical therapy, adaptive physical education, and counseling

SEE ALSO THESE RELATED ENTRIES:

GETTING INVOLVED IN YOUR CHILD'S EDUCATION

Natalie J. Allen, Charles L. Wood,
Susan M. Silvestri, Michelle A. Anderson,
Corinne M. Murphy, and William L. Heward

ALMOST all parents want to be involved in their children's education, but as a parent of a child with an autism spectrum disorder (ASD), your involvement is more critical and requires some additional responsibilities. This includes communicating with your child's teacher, advocating for individualized and effective instruction and services, and actively participating in the instruction your child receives. This entry describes some important steps you can take and strategies you can use to become more involved in your child's education.

BENEFITS OF PARENT INVOLVEMENT

When you become involved in your child's education, you establish a partnership with the professionals who work with your child. By working closely and collaborating with your child's teachers, you can identify meaningful goals and effective strategies to meet them. You can increase consistency between home and school, as well as encourage generalization of skills learned in both settings. When you are involved in your child's education, teachers and service providers can offer knowledge and resources that help you to participate as a full member of your child's educational team. In addition, regular communication with your child's teacher will help you to be better informed about what and how your child is learning in school, and you will be better prepared to participate in educational decisions.

GET TO KNOW YOUR CHILD'S TEACHER

Getting to know your child's teacher and the school staff is the first step in becoming involved in your child's education. Call ahead and schedule a visit with the teacher at a time that is convenient for her or him. Ask about the teacher's educational background and interests, the structure and schedule in the classroom, and his or her expectations of parents. Give the teacher any information that will help him or her to know and educate you and your child.

Take advantage of activities throughout the school year that contribute to a working relationship with your child's teacher and other school staff, such as parent education workshops, teacher appreciation days, open houses, and Parent Teacher Association (PTA) meetings.

VISIT AND PARTICIPATE IN
YOUR CHILD'S CLASSROOM

One of the best ways to stay involved in and informed about your child's education is to visit her or his classroom on a regular basis. Contact the teacher and find out if you can help in the classroom in any way. Teachers appreciate offers and often are looking for assistance in preparing materials for their classes. Volunteer to be the "room parent" or serve on the PTA for the school. Be willing to go on field trips and help out with class parties. Get to know the parents of some of the other students in the class, and discuss ways that you can help the teacher meet the needs of the students he or she is serving.

MAKE PARENT-TEACHER CONFERENCES COUNT

Part of becoming involved in your child's education is attending and actively participating in parent-teacher conferences. Most schools hold conferences once during each grading period. To get the most out of meetings with your child's teacher, arrive prepared to participate actively in the conference. The following is a list of some questions to ask:

- Can I see my child's work?
- What progress is my child making? How do you assess progress?
- What kind of instruction has been most effective with my child?
- What can we do at home to further my child's progress?

Also be sure to offer any information that might be of assistance to your child's teacher. Conclude the meeting by summarizing the information you received and the steps that will be taken to further your child's learning, and set a date for the next conference, if appropriate.

MAINTAIN COMMUNICATION THROUGHOUT THE YEAR

Discuss methods of communication with your child's teacher. Ask him or her if there is an existing communication system in place in the classroom, or work out a method that is both informative and convenient for both of you. Many possible methods of communication exist, including

- phone calls or phone messages,
- e-mail or a class Web site, and
- a daily log book that travels with your child to and from school.

WORK WITH YOUR CHILD AT HOME

You are your child's first teacher. Your child spends more time with you than he or she does with any of the professionals who provide educational services. When you work with your child at home, select skills and goals that are appropriate for the home environment, such as requesting preferred items during play or meals or completing hygiene tasks. Talk with your child's teacher to determine appropriate goals and teaching methods.

EDUCATE YOURSELF

Learn all you can about how to help your child learn. Attend and participate in parent education and support meetings. Get to know the parents of other children in your child's classroom. Ask your child's teacher to recommend print and Internet materials that will contribute to your understanding of how best to educate and advocate for your child.

CONTRIBUTE TO IEP MEETINGS

Individualized Education Program (IEP) meetings are held annually to review and revise your child's goals. The IEP team includes you, your child's teacher, a general education teacher, an individual who can interpret the results of any evaluations that were conducted, and a representative of the school district, as well as other individuals who have knowledge or expertise that applies to your child. You are a full member of this team, and being an active participant in the development of your child's IEP is vital. You can increase your level of involvement by preparing for the IEP meeting in advance. Consider and be prepared to discuss the following items:

- your child's strengths,
- your child's weaknesses,
- any observations you have made of your child's behavior in class or at home, and
- goals you want your child to accomplish in the coming year and in the next few years.

As the parent of a child with an ASD, you have an overwhelming responsibility. The best way to meet this challenge is to become involved in your child's education. Learn all you can about your child's educational strengths and goals, and establish a collaborative relationship with all of the professionals who work with your child. Building an alliance with teachers and other service providers is the best way to advocate for your child.

PRINT RESOURCE

Heward, W. L. (2003). *Exceptional children: An introduction to special education* (7th ed.). Upper Saddle River, NJ: Merrill/Prentice Hall.

KEY TERMS

PARENT TEACHER ASSOCIATION (PTA): A voluntary organization of parents, teachers, and school staff engaged in fund-raising and other activities relating to a school

PARENT-TEACHER CONFERENCE: A meeting between the parent and a teacher—and possibly involving other school staff—to discuss issues related to a child

INDIVIDUALIZED EDUCATION PROGRAM (IEP): A document detailing a child's needs and strengths, as well as what the school will be responsible for teaching during a specified amount of time

SEE ALSO THESE RELATED ENTRIES:

〉

CONTRIBUTING TO EDUCATIONAL PLANNING: A PARENT'S GUIDE TO SUCCESS

E. Amanda Boutot

SINCE its beginning in 1975, and in subsequent revisions, the Individuals with Disabilities Education Act (IDEA) has mandated that families be an integral part of their child's education planning. Often the question that parents have is not *whether* to be involved but *how* to be involved in the planning process for their child's education. This entry addresses how parents can contribute to the planning of their child's education in the public schools by answering some common questions related to family involvement in educational planning.

WHO KNOWS BEST?

All parents want the very best for their children, but how do parents know that what they want is something that the school can provide? Some parents feel that school personnel should make the decisions because of their extensive knowledge in special education and autism. Other parents feel that they, as persons who spend the most time with the child and have known him or her longest, should make most of the decisions. Which is the correct viewpoint? The answer is both. Although the school does have the knowledge and experience in special education that the family may not, it is the family who knows the child best. Therefore, both areas of expertise should be respected and represented in the educational planning process.

WHAT IF I AM NEW TO ALL OF THIS?

Parents interested in becoming more involved in their child's education may find it difficult to make suggestions because they don't know much about the special education system. Therefore, I highly recommend that parents spend time reading over the parent handbook that should be given by the school district to every parent of a child with a disability. If your school has not given you one, ask for it. In addition, do not hesitate to ask questions if the information that you read in this handbook is confusing; set a time to meet with your child's teacher or the school administrator to get clarification on items that are unclear. In addition, many states and local communities have agencies or organizations that provide free advocacy services to families of children with disabilities; some are specifically for families of children with autism. These advocacy services may include an explanation of parental rights in special education, information about autism, and information about educational practices that are considered best. Some agencies will have staff members who can accompany families to the Individualized Education Program (IEP) meeting, to make sure that the family feels comfortable with decisions that are made. One other source of useful information is the Internet. Many Web sites contain information on best practices for children with autism, as well as information about special education services and processes. Parents should become as informed as they possibly can about their child's disability so that they can meaningfully contribute to the planning process.

HOW CAN I CONTRIBUTE?

According to IDEA, parents are equal stakeholders in the planning of their child's educational program; as such, they have protected rights under the law. One recommendation for becoming more involved in planning is for parents to meet with teachers prior to the IEP meeting to discuss their personal ideas and desires concerning their child's education and to see how these are reflected in what the school has in mind. This can be a good opportunity for everyone to have a voice in the process in a relaxed and unofficial manner. Many teachers have family information forms that ask questions (e.g., What does the family do on weekends? What is the child able to do at home and in the community?) and that parents can complete prior to the meeting so that school staff can get to know the child and the family a bit better. Even if your school does not have such a form, it is a good idea to keep track of some of these things yourself so you can offer this very useful information to the school at the time of planning. The following is some information you may want to keep track of and share:

- How does your child communicate his or her wants and needs at home?
- When your child becomes upset or frustrated, what behaviors does he or she display?
- What everyday skills (e.g., dressing, eating) is your child able to do independently? Which ones is he or she able to do with help?

- How do people in your family handle behavioral problems in the home?
- How does your child show affection to family members?
- What games or activities does your family do that your child with autism enjoys?

It also is wise to note areas to address in the educational program that will help your child become more independent at home (e.g., dressing, taking care of belongings, dealing with tantrums). Some families invite the IEP team to their home to assess the needs of the child in that setting so that the IEP is sure to address both home and school needs. Parents must contribute to the educational plan for their child, but they should do so in the ways that feel most comfortable to them.

SUMMARY

Parents are required by law to participate in their child's educational programming (e.g., development of the IEP). The degree of this participation depends largely on the parents themselves. Parents should strive to be well informed regarding autism and the special education process prior to meeting with school staff. Parents might consider meeting with teachers prior to the official IEP meeting to discuss their hopes and dreams for the child, their educational wants and needs, and how to help their child transfer learning from home to school. They also can use this "premeeting" to be sure that school staff has all of the information they need (e.g., the child's abilities, his or her interests at home) to create the most appropriate educational plan possible. Parents should try to come to any meeting with school personnel with lists of information and questions so that their voices can be heard. Being well informed and having useful information to add to the discussion will help parents contribute to their child's education in a meaningful and productive way.

WEB RESOURCE

The Council for Exceptional Children (http://www.cec.sped.org)

KEY TERMS

IEP TEAM: Must include at least one parent; the child's teacher; an administrator or other entity representing the school; any related services personnel such as speech-language pathologists or occupational or physical therapists; and a school psychologist, where appropriate; in addition, anyone else whom the family or the school feels should be present may attend the meeting

INDIVIDUALIZED EDUCATION PROGRAM (IEP): Developed by a team of individuals who are "stakeholders" in a given child's education; an annual plan for what and how a child with a disability will be taught; includes a statement of the child's current abilities, as well as an annual statement of needs. Benchmark objectives also are included and specifically address what will be taught, by whom, and how often it will be evaluated

INDIVIDUALS WITH DISABILITIES EDUCATION ACT (IDEA): Originally passed in 1975, provides procedural safeguards to protect families and children with disabilities; it also requires that parents be contributing members of the IEP team

SEE ALSO THESE RELATED ENTRIES:

PROGRAMS FOR YOUNG CHILDREN WITH AUTISM

EARLY INTERVENTION SERVICES

Jan Butz

WHEN a child under the age of 3 years is identified as having autism, parents can seek early intervention services that specifically address diverse needs. These early intervention services should include both home-based services and some center-based options so that the child can be around other children in preparation for the school-based services offered to students with autism and related disabilities when they are 3 years old. The needs of the family and their priorities for their child should be carefully assessed using a team approach, with input from professionals, such as an occupational therapist, speech-language pathologist, early intervention specialist, psychologist, and medical personnel.

WHAT ARE THE CRITICAL FEATURES OF EFFECTIVE INTERVENTION?

The National Research Council (Lord & McGee, 2001) made several recommendations regarding the characteristics of effective interventions:

- entry into intervention programs/services as soon as a diagnosis of an autism spectrum disorder is being seriously considered;
- active engagement in intensive instructional programming according to the child's chronological age and developmental level;
- repeated, planned teaching opportunities with sufficient amounts of adult attention in one-to-one and very-small-group instruction to meet the child's individualized goals;
- inclusion of a family component with parent training;
- low student-to-teacher ratios; and
- evidence of ongoing program evaluation of a child's progress, with adjustments in programming made on a regular basis.

HOW DO I CHOOSE THE TYPE OF SERVICES THAT IS RIGHT FOR MY CHILD?

The characteristics of the most appropriate intervention for your child must be linked to his or her needs and those of the family. The team who participated in the evaluation of your child should be able to help you decide which type of services will best meet both sets of needs. Just as your family's needs change over time, so will your child's. Ongoing program evaluation and assessment of your child's progress will help you determine what type of services will be the most appropriate at any given time. The curriculum and strategies used across programs will vary in a number of ways, as will strategies and techniques within programs. Some programs adopt the use of one set of procedures, while others will employ a combination of approaches. Programs also will differ in the amount of time that is spent in the home or center.

Home-based services should focus on training family members how to work with the child with autism. This may include behavioral management techniques, use of functional communication systems, and how to set up and implement an in-home behavioral-based program. The last item may involve demonstrating a technique for the parent and then providing feedback as he or she works with the child. The issues that commonly occur in the home often can only be addressed in that setting. These issues may include—but are not limited to—sleep, food, mealtime, toileting, and siblings.

Center-based services focus on working with the children in individualized small- and large-group activities. The emphasis may be on teaching the child how to play appropriately with toys and with other children. Sessions also may focus on how to follow a predictable routine, using visual schedules to promote smooth transitions from one activity to the next. The emphasis may be on teaching children to develop and use their communication and social skills in a group setting.

SUMMARY

When choosing services for your child, you must realize that there can be considerable differences in program philosophies, the techniques or approaches used, and the level of services offered. There also may be distinct differences regarding staffing and ongoing monitoring. As a parent, you should look for early intervention services with certain critical features. Ask yourself, "Does this program or service allow for the implementation of my child's goals as well as our family's goals?" If you are able to answer "yes," you have chosen a program or service that will meet both the child's needs and your family's needs and priorities.

PRINT RESOURCE

Lord, C., & McGee, J. P. (Eds.). (2001). *Educating children with autism.* Washington, DC: National Academy Press.

KEY TERMS

CENTER-BASED SERVICES: Early intervention services provided outside the home in a specialized program, a preschool, or other setting

CURRICULUM: What teachers teach

EARLY INTERVENTION: Specialized services for children with disabilities from birth to 3 years and their families that are provided through Part C of the Individuals with Disabilities Education Act (IDEA)

HOME-BASED SERVICES: Early intervention services provided in the home rather than in a center-based program

SEE ALSO THESE RELATED ENTRIES:

SPEECH THERAPY

Jan Butz

ONE of the primary difficulties young children diagnosed with autism have is a lack of communication skills. According to Wetherby and Prizant (1999), communication goals should focus on the functional use of language and communication in all of the natural settings a child may be in. The speech-language pathologist should not simply teach language and speech behaviors in an isolated setting, such as a therapy room, but rather should focus on helping your child with autism develop a functional communication system.

WHAT DOES YOUR CHILD LIKE?

You should begin teaching your child to use a functional communication system so that his or her basic wants can be met (see Section 4). This will increase your child's willingness to use the system regularly and consistently. As the parent, you know what your child likes to eat or has access to in your home.

You might start this training by writing down a list of items and activities that your child consistently enjoys, including such items as favored foods, toys, activities, or videos. Once you have developed this list, remove your child from the environment so that he or she has limited access to these preferred things throughout the day. A good guideline: If your child can get to the item without asking for it, he or she is more likely to just get it rather than use any communication skills. For instance, if your child can go to the fridge and get a soda, he or she will have no reason to come to you to ask for it.

WHAT DO I TEACH?

The speech-language pathologist's evaluation of your child's communication skills will help in deciding whether to use a verbal communication system or a nonverbal one. Even if your child exhibits some verbal skills, a functional communication system using pictures or icons may be chosen to assist your child in increasing his or her initiation skills or to reduce his or her frustration when trying to communicate with another person. Frost and Bondy (2002), the developers of a functional communication system called the *Picture Exchange Communication System* (PECS), have stated that using this type of system with a child who has limited verbal skills or is considered nonverbal does not prevent the child from learning to speak or speak better. (For a complete description of the PECS system, please refer to http://www.pecs.com or ask your child's speech-language pathologist or other trained professional for additional training on how to progress through the various phases with your child as he or she develops a functional communication system.)

HOW DO I TEACH?

Begin by selecting a time of day when your child is going to make requests to have his or her needs or wants met. For example, parents frequently choose meal and snack times because children often have food items they enjoy and are willing to use a functional communication system to get them. It is best if a third person is available who can serve as a prompter; however, this is not always possible.

Start by breaking the highly preferred food items into several small pieces so that your child will have to make several requests for the item during the training session. Place an icon or photo of the preferred food item on the table or counter between you and your child. Have the food where the child can see it. When he or she reaches for the food icon or photo, physically prompt him or her to pick it up and hand it to you. When your child releases the icon or photo into your hand, quickly respond by giving him or her the actual food item.

ARRANGING FOR OPPORTUNITIES TO COMMUNICATE

Your child's speech–language pathologist will offer suggestions on how to "sabotage" the home setting throughout the day. This means limiting your child's access to activities or items that you know your child would like to have. For instance, if your child really likes trains, you might set up a situation where the train is placed on a high ledge in view but in a place where your child can't reach it without assistance. To get to the train, the child would have to ask for your help in getting the train down by using words such as "train" or "train, please" or giving a photo/icon of the train to you. If your child really likes videos, you might have him or her ask for the video he or she wants prior to turning on the machine. As your child progresses, you should expect the complexity of the language/communication he or she uses to increase. Setting up these situations will seem unnatural at first, but as you begin to see your child more readily using words or a system to communicate wants and needs, you will be able to think of new ways you can modify the home environment to help him or her continue to develop communication for a variety of functions.

SUMMARY

A speech-language pathologist who understands the social and communication problems of children with autism will be a critical member of your child's team. Speech therapy should emphasize the functional use of language and communication in all natural settings. Remember that speech therapy alone in an isolated, unnatural setting will not be enough for your child to develop communication for a variety of functions. The speech-language pathologist should work with you and other team members to address how developing language and communication can be worked into all aspects of the child's day.

REFERENCES

Frost, L., & Bondy, A. (2002). *Picture exchange communication system.* Newark, DE: Pyramid Educational Products.

Wetherby, A., & Prizant, B. (1999). Facilitating language and communication development in autism: Assessment and intervention guidelines. In D. B. Zager (Ed.), *Autism: Identification, education, and treatment* (2nd ed., pp. 107–134). Hillsdale, NJ: Erlbaum.

KEY TERMS

FUNCTIONAL COMMUNICATION: A system or method of communicating with others that allows a person's wants, needs, feelings, or thoughts to be known; usefulness is determined based on how well the person's attempt to communicate is understood by others

PICTURE EXCHANGE COMMUNICATION SYSTEM (PECS): System that uses picture symbols as the primary means of communicating; developed by Lori Frost and Andrew Bondy

SEE ALSO THESE RELATED ENTRIES:

OCCUPATIONAL AND PHYSICAL THERAPY AND THE CHILD WITH AN AUTISM SPECTRUM DISORDER

Yvonne Randall

A CHILD diagnosed with an autism spectrum disorder (ASD) may be referred for physical or occupational therapy as a result of delays identified during a developmental screening or assessment. Physical therapists work with children who have motor difficulties. Occupational therapists work with children who have self-care, motor, cognitive, and social difficulties. Both types of therapy help improve the child's functional performance and enhance his or her ability to interact within the physical and social environments.

PHYSICAL THERAPY

Physical therapy treatment is aimed at developing a child's gross motor skills. The large muscles are used for balance, strength, endurance, coordination, and movement. Physical therapists design gross motor programs incorporating play to help children improve their physical abilities. A treatment session may consist of a child walking, jumping, crawling, or running through an obstacle course. Children with an ASD may exhibit low muscle tone that affects posture and balance. Physical therapists assess the needs of the child and train him or her in the use of crutches, prosthetics, and wheelchairs.

OCCUPATIONAL THERAPY

Occupational therapy treatment focuses on a child's ability to perform in all areas of development, for example, play, cognitive, psychosocial, and self-care skills. Occupational therapy also addresses coping and self-regulation skills and the ability to experience and interpret sensations in the home, school, and community. Occupational therapy interventions can help children develop appropriate social, play, and learning skills. A treatment session may consist of teaching a child how to dress and eat; engaging in play activities to increase trunk, arm, and hand strength; or modifying a classroom so a child can participate with other children. For children with an ASD, the occupational therapist probably will use a *sensory integration approach,* which allows them to actively engage with his or her surroundings to achieve successful adaptive responses or outcomes. Occupational therapists instruct children in the use of adaptive equipment such as wheelchairs, splints, and aids for eating and dressing. They also design or make special equipment needed at home or school.

WHERE DO OCCUPATIONAL AND PHYSICAL THERAPISTS WORK?

Pediatric occupational and physical therapists work in a variety of settings. Hospitals, early intervention programs, school systems, and outpatient rehabilitation clinics are typical places where therapists work with children. Occupational therapists also may work in settings specific to the psychosocial needs of a child.

IMPLEMENTATION OF SERVICES

Physical and occupational therapists should evaluate a child, his or her environment, and the interaction between a child and the environment in a holistic manner. Autism affects each child differently, and a variety of patterns may be seen as children with autism interact with their surroundings. The dynamic nature of this interaction is created in part by the child's continual development, maturation, and learning. As he or she develops and changes, so does the environment. Each therapist will analyze a child's functional performance within different environments to identify his or her strengths and abilities.

Services typically start with a screening to see if therapy would be beneficial. An initial evaluation gathers information about a child's strengths and abilities through interviews, observations, and standardized assessments. Based upon the results of this initial evaluation, the therapist will decide on strategies to guide intervention, including establishing long- and short-term goals. The therapist will reassess your child on a regular basis to see how effective the treatment is and to modify the treatment program as needed.

PRINT RESOURCES

Case-Smith, J. (Ed.). (2001). *Occupational therapy for children* (4th ed.). St. Louis, MO: Mosby.

Hannaford, C. (1995). *Smart moves: Why learning is not all in your head.* Arlington, VA: Great Ocean Publishers.

Kranowitz, C. S. (2002). *The out-of-sync child.* New York: Perigee.

Kranowitz, C. S. (2003). *The out-of-sync child has fun: Activities for kids with sensory integration dysfunction.* New York: Perigee.

Miller-Kuhaneck, H. (Ed.). (2001). *Autism: A comprehensive occupational therapy approach.* Bethesda, MD: American Occupational Therapy Association.

Murray-Slutsky, C., & Paris, B. A. (2000). *Exploring the spectrum of autism and pervasive developmental disorders: Intervention strategies.* San Antonio, TX: Therapy Skill Builders.

WEB RESOURCES

American Occupational Therapy Association (http://www.aota.org)

American Physical Therapy Association (http://www.apta.org)

Neuro-Developmental Treatment Association (http://www.ndta.org)

Sensory Integration Network (http://www.sensoryintegration.org.uk)

KEY TERMS

OCCUPATIONAL THERAPY: A therapy focusing on fine motor skills and sensory integration

PHYSICAL THERAPY: A therapy focusing on gross motor skills and balance

SEE ALSO THESE RELATED ENTRIES:

BEST PRACTICES IN EARLY INTERVENTION AND EARLY CHILDHOOD EDUCATION

Jan Butz

IN 1999, Wetherby and Prizant described "best practices" for educating children with autism spectrum disorders (ASD), and in 2001, the Committee on Educational Intervention for Children with Autism (Lord & McGee, 2001), which had been commissioned by the National Research Council, developed a set of recommendations relating to goals for educational services.

WHAT ARE THE GOALS OF EDUCATIONAL SERVICES?

The goals for educational services for your child with autism should be the same as those for other children: personal independence and social responsibility (Lord & McGee, 2001). These goals suggest that there is a need for continuous progress in social and cognitive abilities, verbal and nonverbal communication skills, adaptive skills, and the reduction of behavioral problems. These abilities and skills should be generalized across a variety of settings. The needs and strengths of children with an ASD are very diverse. The Individualized Family Service Plan (IFSP) and the Individualized Education Program (IEP) should serve as the "blueprint" for planning and implementing the educational objectives that meet your child's specific needs.

What kinds of educational objectives should be on your child's IFSP or IEP? According to the Lord and McGee (2001), they should include the following:

- social skills to increase your child's participation in a variety of activities with peers, family members, and other adults;
- expressive verbal language, receptive language, and nonverbal communication skills;
- a functional communication system;
- increased engagement and flexibility in developmentally appropriate tasks and play, and the ability to attend to the environment and respond to a motivational system;
- fine and gross motor skill development;
- cognitive skills, including play, preacademic, and academic skills;
- replacement of problem behaviors with more appropriate behaviors; and
- independent skills and behaviors that your child will need to succeed in a general education classroom.

Make sure that the objectives developed for your child can be observed and measured. These objectives typically are written for what your child should be able to accomplish within 1 year. Also, measurement of your child's progress toward these educational objectives should occur on a regular basis. This will help you and the other team members decide whether your child is responding and benefiting from a particular intervention. Ongoing assessment and monitoring of your child's educational program will allow team members to make the necessary adjustments so that your child continues to grow and make progress toward the educational goals and objectives identified on his or her IFSP or IEP.

WHAT OTHER "BEST PRACTICES" REGARDING EDUCATING MY CHILD WITH AUTISM SHOULD I LOOK FOR?

Wetherby and Prizant (1999) also noted that communication goals emphasizing the functional use of language and communication across all natural settings are very important. In addition, they suggested that whatever place your child is in should be "engineered" to promote opportunities for your child to communicate with others. Your child will be more successful in a setting that uses environmental supports to promote active and independent participation in activities.

Learning environments that are clearly structured and use predictable routines are examples of essential environmental supports for children with autism. Positive, nonpunitive approaches to problem behaviors are widely accepted as a best practice for children with autism and other disabilities. Teaching replacements for problem behaviors, such as a socially acceptable way to protest or reject, should be addressed and can be included with the communication objectives. If your child will be participating in a general education setting for all or part of the day, the other children in the classroom must be taught how to interact effectively with your child. Finally, your child's level of emotional arousal needs to be watched carefully throughout the day: Situations that are known to upset him or her should be modified, and your child's objectives should include the development of self-regulation skills. For example, your child could be taught to get other individuals' attention when feeling upset or to go to a "quiet" area of the classroom or home.

SUMMARY

Lord and McGee (2001) suggested that appropriate goals are the same for children with autism as they are for other children. Just as other parents want their children to become independent and socially responsible, you have the same goals for your child with autism. Children with autism tend to have very diverse needs. Your child's IEP or IFSP should serve as the "blueprint" for identifying the goals and objectives related to your child's strengths and needs. Your child's educational plan should address several skill areas, and the goals and objectives should be measurable, observable, and frequently monitored so that adjustments can be made.

Wetherby and Prizant (1999) suggested some additional best practices, including using predictable routines, offering structured learning, and teaching other children how to interact effectively with your child. They also suggested that you make sure that your child's level of emotional arousal is watched throughout the day.

REFERENCES

Lord, C., & McGee, J. P. (Eds.). (2001). *Educating children with autism.* Washington, DC: National Academy Press.

Wetherby, A., & Prizant, B. (1999). Facilitating language and communication development in autism: Assessment and intervention guidelines. In D. B. Zager (Ed.), *Autism: Identification, education, and treatment* (2nd ed., pp. 107–134). Hillsdale, NJ: Erlbaum.

KEY TERMS

INDIVIDUALIZED EDUCATION PROGRAM (IEP): Mandated by the Individuals with Disabilities Education Act (IDEA) for all students ages 3–21 years with disabilities in public schools; the plan includes long-term annual goals, short-term or benchmark objectives of what will be taught to the student in a given year, as well as additional information on the child's current levels of performance based on assessments and the type of assessment procedures that will be used to monitor the goals and objectives

INDIVIDUALIZED FAMILY SERVICE PLAN (IFSP): Required by Part C of IDEA for infants and toddlers (ages birth to 3 years) with or at risk for disabilities and their families; includes goals and objectives for the student and services needed by the family

SEE ALSO THESE RELATED ENTRIES:

WHAT IS ABA?

Susan M. Silvestri, Charles L. Wood,
Natalie J. Allen, Michelle A. Anderson,
Corinne M. Murphy, and William L. Heward

WHAT ABA IS

ABA stands for *applied behavior analysis,* a scientific discipline devoted to improving and understanding human behavior. Specifically, ABA focuses on objectively defined, observable behaviors important to daily life. To date, ABA has been the most effective tool for improving outcomes for young children with disabilities.

Several defining characteristics of ABA are described in this entry.

ABA IS INDIVIDUALIZED

In ABA, teaching goals are determined by a careful assessment of the current skills of the individual. Skills to be taught are not selected from a cookbook-type list but rather are determined for each person. Behaviors most likely to produce good outcomes for the child and his or her family are the primary focus of ABA-based teaching.

ABA IS DATA-BASED EVALUATION AND DECISION MAKING

Direct and frequent measurement is the foundation of ABA; therefore, target behaviors are specifically defined. For example, a specific target behavior associated with the goal of communication might be *greeting*, which might be defined as the child responding to another person saying "Hi" by waving. Each recorded instance of waving becomes *data*, which then are used to guide instructional decision making.

ABA IS DESIGNED TO BE EFFECTIVE

Because data are collected directly and frequently during instruction, learning continuously is assessed. By examining the data, teachers and parents easily can determine whether the instruction is working. If the child is not making reasonable progress, instruction should be modified. For example, if a young girl did not wave when others greeted her in at least 8 of 10 trials, the teacher might add a prompt or look at ways to make the instruction more motivating.

When teachers and therapists do not verify the effects of instruction by collecting direct and frequent measurements of their student's performance, they are prone to two mistakes:

1. continuing to use ineffective interventions when no real improvements have occurred (e.g., the therapist falsely believes a certain type of intervention is effective), and
2. discontinuing effective programs because a subjective judgment indicates no improvement.

ABA IS DOABLE

Parents can learn the basic principles of ABA and incorporate teaching strategies based on those principles into their daily interactions with their children. For example, a parent could work on his or her child's greeting behavior throughout the day. Whenever the child encountered a new person, or whenever a parent or sibling greeted the child, they could prompt the child to wave and then praise and reinforce that behavior.

Finally, ABA is, in the words of one mother of a young child with autism, "good old-fashioned hard work." ABA is not a magic bullet or a miracle cure. It requires diligent, continuous observation. Because behavior is always happening, teaching is always happening. When used correctly, ABA can produce meaningful, life-changing results.

WHAT ABA IS NOT

ABA DOES NOT PRESCRIBE INSTRUCTIONAL SETTINGS, TEACHING FORMATS, OR MATERIALS

Because ABA does not dictate any specific type of instructional method or format, the phrase *ABA method* is a misnomer. ABA is broader than any "brand name" method of behaviorally based instruction or therapy (e.g., Lovaas method [Lovaas, 2003], PECS). Many service providers and parents mistakenly believe that ABA is one of these ABA-based brand names; however, branded training is no substitute for in-depth training in applied behavior analysis.

ABA IS NOT BRIBERY

In ABA, every effort is made to increase children's motivation and make learning fun. Naturally occurring consequences are used as reinforcers whenever possible. For example, instead of using edible items when teaching play skills, parents or teachers use naturally occurring consequences, such as access to favorite toys. (*Bribery* involves the use of rewards or payments in an attempt to induce someone to conduct an illegal or otherwise undesirable act.)

ABA IS NOT PUNITIVE

Positive strategies are used until they are exhausted, and rewards are delivered systematically to increase appropriate behavior, which is the goal of ABA. An important element of ABA is to determine the function of a particular behavior. For example, does a child throw a tantrum because he or she wants attention? Does he or she throw things because he or she needs help? Knowing why children demonstrate challenging behaviors allows parents and teachers to teach appropriate replacement behaviors, such as tapping a person on the shoulder to get attention or using spoken words or a communication device to say, "I need help."

QUALITY INDICATORS OF ABA SERVICES

The following are indicators of quality ABA services:
- The curriculum should be individualized and should address skills across a variety of settings.
- Teaching should involve continuous measurement of behavior and data-based decision making.
- The instructional environment should be positive. This means that staff members focus on catching students "being good," avoid reprimands, and use positive reinforcement to teach appropriate behaviors.
- Parent involvement and collaboration should be encouraged and maximized. Parents should be encouraged to visit the classroom or center at any time. ABA providers should (a)

give objective information about their child's progress, (b) encourage parent input for instructional goals, and (c) give parents information and support so they can offer their child learning opportunities at home.

- All instructional staff members should be observed frequently and provided with ongoing feedback on their teaching performance.
- All persons providing ABA services should have completed some type of formal training recognized by a state or national organization. An increasing number of colleges and universities offer programs in ABA. The Behavior Analyst Certification Board provides nationally recognized certification to behavior analysts. Although certification is neither a requirement for, nor a guarantee of quality services, it does tell parents and other consumers that an individual has acquired a standard foundation of knowledge in ABA and has been supervised or mentored while providing ABA services.

REFERENCE

Lovaas, O. I. (2003). *Teaching individuals with developmental delays: Basic intervention techniques.* Austin, TX: PRO-ED.

PRINT RESOURCES

Cooper, J. O., Heron, T. E., & Heward, W. L. (2005). *Applied behavior analysis* (2nd ed.). Upper Saddle River, NJ: Merrill/Prentice Hall.

Maurice, C., Green, G., & Luce, S. C. (1996). *Behavioral intervention for young children with autism: A manual for parents and professionals.* Austin, TX: PRO-ED.

Simpson, R. L. (2001). ABA and students with autism spectrum disorders: Issues and considerations for effective practice. *Focus on Autism and Other Developmental Disabilities, 16,* 68–71.

WEB RESOURCES

Association for Behavior Analysis (http://www.abainternational.org)

Association for Science in Autism Treatment (http://www.asatonline.org)

Behavior Analyst Certification Board (http://www.bacb.com)

Cambridge Center for Behavioral Studies (http://www.behavior.org)

KEY TERMS

APPLIED BEHAVIOR ANALYSIS (ABA): The application of behavioral methods to solve human problems

DATA: Information collected to help in making an educated and informed decision

SEE ALSO THESE RELATED ENTRIES:

FINDING A THERAPIST FOR YOUR CHILD WITH AUTISM

Renee K. Van Norman and Elizabeth C. Rusinko

FINDING a therapist for your child at times can appear to be an overwhelming task. Where do you look? What type of questions do you ask? What makes a good therapist? Fortunately, help is available. This entry is designed to guide you in your search for the most effective therapist for your child. We have also included a template for helping you advertise for a therapist in your area. With some careful planning and diligence, you can find a qualified therapist with the skills necessary to help your child succeed academically, emotionally, and socially.

BEGINNING THE SEARCH

If you have access to a computer, the Internet is an excellent resource for the initial search stages. We suggest starting with a search engine (e.g., Google, Yahoo, etc.) and entering keywords such as *autism, applied behavior analysis,* or *behavioral supports.* You will find many Web sites containing information about autism, some of which will include information related to finding a therapist. These Web sites also can be amazing resources for materials, contacts, and advice.

We also suggest contacting your local library and asking for reference materials that may be specific to your school district, city, or town. The librarian most likely will be the most familiar with the reference materials, which may save you time and money. Your local school district may be able to supply you with information concerning therapist availability. You also can ask your pediatrician, your neighbors, and members of your religious community for the names of organizations that offer therapeutic services. Local universities and colleges also are a great resource for locating therapists for your child. You often can find university students who are highly motivated and well educated in program development for children with autism who are typically eager to find part-time positions while attending school. We suggest you contact the head of the special education, psychology, education, speech or communication disorders, occupational therapy, or physical therapy department at a local university or college in your area; this individual will be able to direct you to the professors whose students would be best qualified to work with your family.

Your local Autism Society chapter is another terrific resource. Membership benefits often will include parent networking and therapist referrals. Many times one therapist will be able to work with two or three families simultaneously. This is a good place to receive referrals for therapists from a satisfied parent. You may find information about your local chapter on the Web (http://www.autism-society.org), at the library, or just by asking some of the parents and professionals at your child's school. Some chapters hold annual conferences where you might network with family members of children with autism to locate a therapist who is a good match for your child. We suggest looking into this resource and becoming a member so that you are provided with up-to-date information on the events, services, and materials available through the society. The Families for Early Autism Treatment (FEAT; http://www.feat.org) organization also has chapters in many communities and is a great place to obtain information on potential therapists for your son or daughter.

Finally, many parents become the primary therapist for their son or daughter's home programming. Before embarking on this tremendous task, however, we suggest that you receive training from a certified behavior analyst with specialization in programming for children with autism. Contact the Behavior Analyst Certification Board (http://www.bacb.com) for a list of all board-certified behavior analysts in the United States. The Cambridge Center for Behavioral Studies Web site (http://www.behavior.org) also has many helpful references in its autism section. With the appropriate levels of support, parents can become highly skilled therapists and provide the necessary teaching for their son or daughter's success. After all, you are with your child many hours of the day and across many different teaching situations. However, you should have individuals who are experienced in programming for children with autism review the curriculum you are using and supervise some of the teaching sessions so that you receive enough feedback on your effectiveness and suggestions for modifications you might make to continue helping your child achieve as much as possible. This can be a rewarding experience for both you and your child.

ADVERTISING FOR A THERAPIST

Advertising in your local newspaper, local college or university paper, or online is another excellent way to find a therapist. Be as specific as possible concerning qualifications, hours, and salary. This will help you speed up the interviewing process because it will help you identify qualified individuals more easily. The following is an example of an advertisement for a therapist:

Position Available: Seeking enthusiastic individuals to work with a team providing intensive early intervention for a child with developmental disabilities. Experience in behavioral therapy helpful but not necessary. We will provide training. Time commitment: 6–10 hours a week. Pay is $–$$, depending upon experience. (Maurice, Green, & Luce, 1996; you should adapt this example to fit your specific requirements)

Distributing flyers throughout your community also is another great way to find a therapist. You can display flyers in your local grocery store, on community bulletin boards, and at your local college or university. Your flyer should include a description of the job, the salary, training requirements, and scheduling restrictions (see Figure 2).

We suggest that you include removable tabs at the bottom of the flyer containing a phone number where interested individuals can contact you. Some parents choose to include a picture of their child on the flyer. Although we have found that it can be a very effective way to gain the attention of potential applicants, parents also must take into consideration privacy and security issues when deciding whether or not to include a photo of their child. Another way to attract a therapist with the right kind of experience is to use text that highlights special characteristics of your child.

Many colleges and universities have their own Web sites that include job postings. You will need to talk to someone in the department in which you are interested to find out the specifics about posting your ad. Some departments even have a listserv

Part-Time Tutor/Therapist Needed

Please join our team and work with a wonderful and energetic 3-year-old child with autism in our Wilmington home using a home-based intervention program based on Applied Behavior Analysis.

Job Description:

- Part-time job providing 4–8 hours a week of one-to-one teaching
- Flexible scheduling
- Wage based on experience
- Mandatory, paid training provided
- Must be available for team meetings

Requirements:

- We are seeking someone who will be dedicated to our child and enthusiastic about working with children with autism.
- The right person will be able to follow directions and accept feedback about programming changes and implementation.
- Education, Special Education, OT/PT, Psychology, Early Childhood, or Speech/Language majors preferred.
- At least 1 year of college completed
- Must have own transportation
- Contact Joe or Sally Smith at 555-5555 on weekdays between 4 p.m. and 8 p.m.

Part-Time Tutor/Therapist — Call Joe or Sally Smith — 555-5555

Part-Time Tutor/Therapist — Call Joe or Sally Smith — 555-5555

Part-Time Tutor/Therapist — Call Joe or Sally Smith — 555-5555

Part-Time Tutor/Therapist — Call Joe or Sally Smith — 555-5555

Part-Time Tutor/Therapist — Call Joe or Sally Smith — 555-5555

Part-Time Tutor/Therapist — Call Joe or Sally Smith — 555-5555

FIGURE 2. Template for a flyer to advertise for a part-time tutor/therapist.

to which all of their students subscribe. These departments may allow you to send an advertisement out over the listserv to recruit therapists. There usually is no charge for doing this.

SELECTING A GOOD THERAPIST

Prior to setting an interview, we suggest speaking with the person on the phone. The following list contains some questions you might want to ask:

- Do you have previous experience working with children with autism?
- Have you taken any classes or have you attended any training sessions in programming curriculum for children with autism?
- Are you familiar with discrete trial training or early intensive behavioral therapy?
- Are you willing and able to participate in team meetings and provide feedback regarding your sessions with my child?

Obviously, applicants who answer "yes" to these questions are preferable; however, a potential candidate may not have the background and training you desire but may express a willingness to learn. In our opinion, this willingness to learn is an excellent quality in a potential therapist and is something you should be looking for in any individual planning to work with your child.

Because the therapist you choose will be working closely with your family and may be working in your home, be sure to thoroughly check references; conduct background checks, if necessary; and talk at length with any candidates about goals that you have for your son or daughter. You should feel comfortable with having this person in your home to work closely with your child. Before hiring anyone as part of your team, we recommend having the candidate work or play with your son or daughter for at least 20 minutes while you observe him or her. You will be able to see how he or she interacts with your child. You can thus get at least a preliminary sense of the teaching style that the therapist uses in conducting sessions. If you are hiring a therapist to work in your child's classroom rather than in your home, be sure to check with staff members from your school district to find out what type of interview process they may have. Also, be sure to find out whether they would like to be present at the interview to collaborate with you on making a hiring decision.

PAYING FOR SERVICES

Paying for these specialized services can be expensive. Most of the time, you do not need to pay the entire cost. Funding sources vary across school districts, so we suggest you contact your district early in your search for a therapist and inquire about program options. Some school districts have their own services and therapists, and these therapists may be a good fit with your child's particular programming needs. In addition, some insurance carriers are willing to pay for ABA therapy.

REFERENCE

Maurice, C., Green, G., & Luce, S. C. (1996). *Behavioral intervention for young children with autism: A manual for parents and professionals.* Austin, TX: PRO-ED.

PRINT RESOURCES

Scott, J. (1996). Recruiting, selecting, and training teaching assistants. In C. Maurice, G. Green, & S. Luce (Eds.), *Behavioral intervention for young children with autism* (pp. 231–240). Austin, TX: PRO-ED.

Shook, G. L., & Favell, J. (1996). Identifying qualified professionals in behavior analysis. In C. Maurice, G. Green, & S. Luce (Eds.), *Behavioral intervention for young children with autism* (pp. 221–230). Austin, TX: PRO-ED.

Wright, P., & Wright, P. (2001). *Wrightslaw: Special education law.* Hartfield, VA: Harbor House Law Press.

Wright, P., & Wright, P. (2002). *From emotions to advocacy: The special education survival guide.* Hartfield, VA: Harbor House Law Press.

WEB RESOURCES

Behavior Books (http://www.behaviorbooks.org)

The Cambridge Center for Behavioral Studies (http://www.behavior.org)

KEY TERMS

ABA THERAPY: Proactive approaches and specific strategies designed to teach specific skills and improve behavior

DISCRETE TRIAL INSTRUCTION: Teaching a single skill or part of a skill

SEE ALSO THESE RELATED ENTRIES:

SECTION
4

ISSUES IN COMMUNICATION

DEVELOPING YOUR CHILD'S SPEECH: "WILL MY CHILD LEARN TO TALK?"

Matt Tincani

PARENTS of children with an autism spectrum disorder (ASD) often ask, "Will my child talk?" This is a good question, because children with an ASD often have speech delays. Unfortunately, there is no straightforward answer. Research has suggested that many adults with autism—as many as half—do not have functional speech. The outlook is not as bad as it appears, however. Research also has told us that some of these children who receive intervention that includes speech instruction may learn to talk. Learning to use an augmentative and alternative communication (AAC) system also may promote speech. As a parent, there are a number of things that you can do to help develop your child's speech.

THE DIFFERENCE BETWEEN SPEECH AND COMMUNICATION

Before you begin, you should know the difference between speech and communication. *Speech* describes the vocal sounds we use to talk. *Communication* describes the behavior we engage in to produce the attention of another person. Not all speech is communication. For example, children with autism sometimes repeat the last word or phrase they hear. A child might hear the word "candy" on the TV and then say, "candy." This is called *echolalia,* which usually is not communication because it does not involve getting another person's attention. When your child says, "candy" to you and gets candy, this is communication because he or she is getting your attention to obtain a desired item. Teaching communication is very important for children with autism; therefore, you should make sure that the speech your child develops helps him or her communicate with others.

DEVELOPING SPEECH FOR A CHILD WHO CAN IMITATE SOME WORDS OR SOUNDS

Some children with autism can imitate some sounds, words, and sentences. You may know that your child can imitate because you have heard him or her making sounds such as "ba-ba" or "ma-ma" in response to someone saying "baby" or "mama." If you are uncertain about your child's imitative skills, you might informally test the skills by saying some simple, one-syllable sounds (e.g., "ma," "ka," "da," "ba") to see if he or she will imitate them. If your child can successfully imitate these one-syllable sounds, you then might try simple words (e.g., "baby," "mommy," "daddy," "doggie"). If he or she can imitate sounds or words, you can use these imitation skills to develop more speech.

STEP 1: IDENTIFY PREFERRED ITEMS

It will be easier to develop your child's speech if you use items and activities that he or she likes. You may begin by making a list of 10–12 favorite things, including edibles (e.g., fruits, candy, snacks), drinks, toys, and activities (e.g., tickles, singing). It is better to start with things that can be given discretely (i.e., over and over again in a short time period). For example, a banana cut up into small pieces, small sips of a drink from a cup, or a hand-sized toy such as a top.

STEP 2: SELECT A TIME OF DAY

Select a time of day when you can spend at least 10–20 minutes working with your child on speech. You might select a meal or snack time, play time, or other nondemanding time. Have the preferred items within reach. Present one item or activity to your child at a time. It is a good idea to give him or her "free" access at least one time before you begin to teach. If your child appears to want the item or to enjoy the activity, you may start teaching. If, on the other hand, he or she does not like the item/activity or pushes it away, pick something else.

STEP 3: PRESENT, PROMPT, AND PRAISE

Present the item or activity again, except this time say the first syllable of the name as you present it. For example, if you are presenting a ball, say the "ba" sound as you give it to your child. If he or she attempts to imitate—or successfully imitates—the sound, provide lavish praise (e.g., "Great job! You said ba!"). If your child does not attempt to imitate, you may prompt by saying the sound again one or two times. Be sure to give your child the item quickly (i.e., within 2 seconds), even if he or she does not imitate. At this early stage of teaching, you must not withhold the item for too long. Doing so for more than 1–2 seconds may frustrate your child and turn her or him off to speech entirely. After you have presented one item a few times, switch to another item, and then another. This will help maintain interest. Until your child begins to reliably imitate your sounds, use only a few items.

STEP 4: GRADUALLY DELAY YOUR PROMPTS

Once your child is able to reliably say the first syllable of a word, you may begin to delay your prompts. You do this by presenting an item or activity and waiting a second before you deliver the prompt. If your child "beats" the prompt or says the sound before you, immediately give him or her the item and provide enthusiastic praise. When you praise, you should repeat the sound (e.g., "You're right! That's ba!"). You may gradually increase the delay by up to 4 seconds. Again, watch for signs of frustration. If your child consistently waits for you to prompt or gets upset when you withhold an item, you should keep the delay very short (i.e., less than 1 second). If your child learns to say a number of sounds without prompts, you may try prompting for a lengthier approximation of the name or the entire name of the item or activity.

DEVELOPING COMMUNICATION FOR A CHILD WHO CANNOT IMITATE WORDS OR SOUNDS

Some children with autism have a difficult time imitating speech. Trying to develop speech for them in the manner described above may lead to frustration. Although developing speech is important, your child also needs to learn to communicate. A number of AAC systems—such as picture-based systems, sign language, and voice-output devices—are available for children who cannot use functional speech. If your child cannot imitate sounds, you should implement one of these systems before you try to develop speech by itself.

Naturalistic teaching consists of teaching strategies used in everyday settings, such as the home. To conduct naturalistic teaching, you should observe your child in a natural setting such as the playroom or kitchen. You should stand a few feet away, watching to see what your child finds to be interesting in the room. If he or she reaches for a toy or opens the refrigerator to get a drink, briefly block access to the desired item and prompt her or him to say the name of the item, using the teaching procedures described earlier. If he or she is not yet able to say the name of the item, prompt for an approximation of the name (e.g., the "j" sound for juice). Remember to give your child access to the item quickly, regardless of whether he or she imitates your prompt. If your child is beginning to comment on things in the place, you also may use naturalistic teaching to develop speech. For example, if your child points outside the window and says "car," praise him or her lavishly and repeat the word (e.g., "Great job, that is a car!"). If he or she says an approximation of the word (e.g., "ca" instead of "car"), praise her or him lavishly and prompt for the entire word. The more you encourage your child to speak across the day, the greater the likelihood that he or she will learn to speak.

PRINT RESOURCES

Koegel, R. L., & Koegel, L. K. (1995). *Teaching children with autism: Strategies for initiating positive interactions and improving learning opportunities.* Baltimore: Brookes.

Maurice, C., Green, G., & Luce, S. C. (1996). *Behavioral intervention for young children with autism: A manual for parents and professionals.* Austin, TX: PRO-ED.

Sundberg, M. L., & Partington, J. W. (1998). *Teaching language to children with autism or other developmental disabilities.* Danville, CA: Behavior Analysts.

KEY TERMS

AUGMENTATIVE AND ALTERNATIVE COMMUNICATION (AAC): Systems available for children who cannot use functional speech; they include picture-based systems, sign language, and voice output devices

ECHOLALIA: Repeating the last word or phrase the child hears; not usually communication because it does not involve another person acting as a listener

NATURALISTIC TEACHING: Describes strategies to encourage speech in everyday settings, including the home

PROMPT: Aiding the child; for example, if presenting a ball, saying the "ba" sound as a prompt

SEE ALSO THESE RELATED ENTRIES:

AUGMENTATIVE AND ALTERNATIVE COMMUNICATION

Laura Lacey Rismiller

WHAT IS AUGMENTATIVE AND ALTERNATIVE COMMUNICATION (AAC)?

Augmentative and alternative communication is any communication that requires the use of *something other than a person's own body* (Cook & Hussey, 1995). For example, a person with cerebral palsy who does not communicate vocally may point to letters or symbols on a board to communicate his or her wants or needs. Devices can either be manual (e.g., paper and pencil, switches) or electronic (e.g., typewriter, computer, other electronic devices); however, both types of AAC require a symbol system and a way to select the symbols.

WHO USES AAC DEVICES?

AAC devices are used by people with a wide variety of disabilities, including

- persons with language and communication disorders (e.g., autism, pervasive developmental disorders [PDD]);
- persons with visual or hearing disabilities; and

- persons with limited motor capabilities (e.g., cerebral palsy, spina bifida).

TYPES OF AAC

All types of AAC share two similar characteristics: a specific symbol system and a method of selection.

1. *Unaided communication:* This is any communication that requires a person to use only his or her body. Examples include sign language or finger spelling and pointing (includes head and mouth pointers).

2. *Low-tech/manual communication:* This is any communication aid that is inexpensive, relatively simple to make or create, and effortless to obtain. Examples include the following:
   - paper and pencil;
   - picture boards;
   - Picture Exchange Communication System (PECS; Frost & Bondy, 2002), a system where persons may exchange a piece of paper with a symbol on it to communicate a want or need; and
   - stamps.

3. *High-tech/electronic communication:* This is any communication that requires a multifaceted system and often is difficult to create or obtain due to its cost and complexity. Examples include the following:
   - text-to-speech programs, which analyze and translate words and sentences using codes and speech synthesizers;

- voice-output devices, which produce sounds in the forms of words or sentences when a person selects a specific symbol or sequence of symbols; and
- computer software, which are programs that run on computers and allow individuals to use keyboards or switches to communicate.

4. The following Web sites may assist you in finding the appropriate AAC:
   - ABLEDATA (http://www.abledata.com)
   - Augmentative Communication, Inc. (http://www.augcominc.com)
   - Mayer-Johnson, Inc. (http://www.mayer-johnson.com)

CONSIDERATIONS FOR SELECTING AAC

The following questions should be considered when selecting AAC:

1. *Is it age appropriate?* Select an AAC that is age appropriate for the individual.
2. *What are the required skills?* Select an AAC that is appropriate to the skill level of the individual. For example, if a person does not have the skills necessary for using the PECs (e.g., fine motor skill of grasping), it would not be appropriate for him or her.
3. *Is it practical?* Be sure to look at the number of steps required to use the AAC and what those steps actually look like. Are there too many? Is it practical? These questions should be addressed during the AAC training.
4. *What about the future?* Look at the individual's long-term goals and make sure that the AAC fits with those goals.

FUNDING TIPS AND RESOURCES
FOR PARENTS AND CAREGIVERS

The following tips will help parents and caregivers select an AAC:

1. Make sure that you know what your rights are according to the law. Go online, read related books and articles, and talk to everyone you can to find out as much information as possible about AAC.

2. Know that you are your child's best advocate and best hope for obtaining what he or she needs to communicate more effectively.

3. Know your child's strengths and abilities and select an AAC accordingly. Familiarize yourself with various technologies by asking questions and talking to teachers, speech-language pathologists, and physical or occupational therapists.

4. Contact specific agencies as funding sources for AAC.
   - Medicare is a federal program that provides health care for people ages 65 and older and also for individuals receiving Social Security disability benefits; however, their coverage for AAC devices is extremely limited.
   - Medicaid is a state/federal program that provides health care to individuals and families with low incomes. A physician must prescribe an AAC device as a "medically necessary treatment" for it to be covered by Medicaid.
   - Private insurance funds vary greatly, depending on the company. Insurance companies usually will pay for items such as wheelchairs or scooters with proper documentation or prescriptions; however, most companies will challenge or deny claims when the cost is more than what is "standard and customary." There

seems to be no set procedure or protocol for dealing with coverage for AAC devices.

- There are many private funding sources for which you may write letters or grants to receive money for AAC devices. These can be found through attending workshops, contacting local organizations, and going online.

REFERENCES

Cook, A. M., & Hussey, S. M. (1995). *Assistive technologies: Principles and practices*. St. Louis, MO: Mosby.

Frost, L., & Bondy, A. (2002). *Picture exchange communication system*. Newark, DE: Pyramid Educational Products.

WEB RESOURCES

ABLEDATA (http://www.abledata.com)

The Alliance for Technology Access (ATA; http://www.ataccess.org)

Center for Information Technology Accommodation (CITA; http://www.icdri.org/MethandTech.htm)

Family Center on Technology and Disability (http://www.fctd.info)

United Cerebral Palsy Associations, Inc. (http://www.ucp.org)

KEY TERMS

AUGMENTATIVE AND ALTERNATIVE COMMUNICATION (**AAC**): Any communication that uses something other than speech

PICTURE EXCHANGE COMMUNICATION SYSTEM (**PECS**): An AAC system using picture symbols

SEE ALSO THESE RELATED ENTRIES:

PICTURE-BASED COMMUNICATION SYSTEMS

Tabitha J. Kirby, Jennifer Migliorini, and Stephanie Peterson

PICTURE-BASED communication systems are a great way to teach communication to children with a diagnosis on the autism spectrum. Most children with autism and related disorders have very strong visual skills and a greater ability to learn visually. A picture communication system uses the child's strengths to teach him or her a powerful way to get his or her needs met. Some children can pull a parent to a desired item, some can point to what they want, and some children cry until the parent figures out what the desired item is. All of these children can express what they desire by seeing the item; therefore, all of these children could communicate with pictures.

The ability to communicate also is highly motivating to your child. Communicating through pictures allows him or her to ask for items or breaks and to indicate needs in a way that nearly always results in (a) less time spent trying to tell an adult what he or she wants, and (b) getting the correct item more often. Communication also allows your child to begin to socially interact with others. Picture systems are easily understood and thus provide a way for persons to interact with your child in return.

Not only is it wonderful to provide a way of temporary communication, but a child who can learn to talk will learn, if the system is used correctly and in the same way every time.

WHAT ARE PICTURE-BASED COMMUNICATION SYSTEMS?

Picture-based communication systems use pictures that are set up and taught in such a way that a child can communicate needs and wants and eventually comment and ask questions. There are many different types of picture systems that fall into two broad categories: low tech and high tech. We will discuss both.

WHAT ARE LOW-TECH COMMUNICATION SYSTEMS?

Low-tech systems are nonelectronic and usually consist of some sort of board or notebook with pictures. Examples include communication boards, communication books, schedule boards, and conversation books. The child points to, touches, or gives someone a picture indicating what he or she is trying to tell that person. These systems can be made at home and generally are relatively inexpensive, portable, and durable. They do lack an audio component, however.

One well-known type of low-tech system is the *Picture Exchange Communication System* (PECS; Frost & Bondy, 2002). In fact, picture-based communication systems often are erroneously referred to as PECS. PECS is a specific curriculum for teaching picture-based communication that systematically moves the child from requesting to commenting, using descriptive words, and asking and answering questions.

Other low-tech systems use pictures in a board, book, or schedule format. A board allows all pictures to be displayed at once. A book could be sorted by type of picture (e.g., foods, toys, places) or have one or a few pictures per page. A schedule could consist of planned activities or several choices of activities. Any type of communication board or book consisting of pictures that are of value to your child's life could be made at home. You can adapt the PECS format of teaching to the device being used.

WHAT ARE HIGH-TECH COMMUNICATION SYSTEMS?

High-tech simply means that the system is electronic. Nonverbal children and adults use several varieties of high-tech systems for communication. Generally, these systems employ some type of picture presentation with an accompanying audio output for each picture. For example, when the child touches the picture of milk, a prerecorded message, "I want milk, please," plays. Most systems are highly portable. These types of systems make communication possible with most anyone.

Several systems provide a smaller display of pictures, are more cost-effective, and are easily portable. One of these systems, the Parakeet, offers a small display of pictures (5–15) with more than 5 seconds of recording time for each picture. This machine is simple to set up and easy to use and is very lightweight. Another system, the Advocate, displays 1, 2, 4, 8, or 16 pictures with 16 minutes of recording time. This system also is very portable. Another small, simple-to-use system, the CheapTalk8, features an 8-picture display with 5 seconds of recording time per picture. Other smaller systems include The Pathfinder, Dynavox, Dynamyte, Palm-Top Portable IMPACT, and Springboard.

A more complex and expensive type of electronic picture-based communication system is the Vantage, which provides a larger display of pictures or letters and allows for longer recorded messages. This type of system is more difficult to program and may be more time consuming to use at first. Another system that is more complex is the MACAW family of devices. These larger machines are less portable and, like the Vantage, are more costly.

HOW DO I CHOOSE?

Choosing a communication system to use with your child may seem overwhelming. Here are some questions you should ask yourself before making a selection:

1. Where will the system be used?
2. Who needs to be trained on the system?
3. Is training provided?
4. How much recording time is needed?
5. What should the life of the battery be?
6. How is it transported?
7. Is it easy for my child to use?
8. Will it meet my child's needs?

REFERENCE

Frost, L., & Bondy, A. (2002). *Picture exchange communication system.* Newark, DE: Pyramid Educational Products.

WEB RESOURCES

Ability Hub Assistive Technology Solutions (http://abilityhub.com)

Augmentative Communication, Inc. (http://www.augcominc.com)

Beyond Play (http://www.beyondplay.com)

LAB Resources (http://www.elabresources.com)

Mayer-Johnson, Inc. (http://www.mayer-johnson.com)

Pyramid Educational Consultants (http://www.pecs.com)

Zygo Industries, Inc. (http://www.zygo-usa.com/products.htm)

KEY TERMS

Audio component: Provides verbal examples for the child every time he or she communicates with pictures

High-tech system: Picture-based communication system that is electronic and provides prerecorded messages for each picture

Low-tech system: Picture-based communication system that is not electronic and can easily be made in the home

Picture Exchange Communication System (PECS): Using a book with pictures; a low-tech system that provides a set curriculum for teaching communication with pictures

Picture-based communication system: Many different types of systems that allow for a variety of display; may be low- or high-tech devices that are used to communicate with others

SEE ALSO THESE RELATED ENTRIES:

SIGN LANGUAGE

Matt Tincani

Despite our best efforts, many children with autism have difficulty learning to talk. Augmentative and alternative communication (AAC) may be appropriate for these children. In AAC training, a child is taught how to communicate in a way other than through speech. For example, he or she may be taught to exchange a picture or press a button on a voice output device to make his or her needs and wants known to others. *Sign language* is another form of AAC that is appropriate for some children. A child who uses sign language forms hand signs to request preferred items or to perform other language functions. This entry describes how to teach sign language to a nonverbal child with autism. (*Note.* When we use "sign language," we are not referring to American Sign Language, per se, but any kind of understood hand signs to represent words and phrases.)

TEACHING SIGN LANGUAGE

WHAT DOES YOUR CHILD LIKE?

Begin sign language training by teaching your child to request things that he or she likes, which will increase her or his motivation to use sign language. You know your child's likes—for example, juice, tickles, hugs, toys—and dislikes—for example, loud noises, changes in routine, unpleasant activities. You might start by making a list of 5–10 items that your child enjoys consistently. Try to select things that can be accessed for a short period of time, such as small pieces of candy, sips of juice, tickles, and hand toys like balls or tops. Also try to select things that can be given repeatedly in a short period of time. When you begin teaching, limit your child's access to these things for about an hour before you begin. Limiting access increases the likelihood that he or she will be motivated to make a request during teaching.

WHAT DO I TEACH?

To prevent your child from becoming confused, begin by teaching one sign for one preferred item or activity. As he or she learns to use this sign, you may introduce another sign, and so on. Teach signs that are *iconic* (resemble the things they represent). For example, the sign for ball is forming your hands in the shape of a ball in front of you. It also is a good idea to teach signs that are simple to perform. Try to avoid signs that require your child to make hand or finger motions. There are a number of commercially available sign language books and dictionaries. You also may find interactive sign language dictionaries on the Internet.

HOW DO I TEACH?

To begin, select a time of day during which you can spend 10–20 minutes with your child. Any room of the house is fine, as long as the TV, toys, siblings, and other distractions are not present. Start by presenting a small amount of the preferred item or activity. This means giving a bite-size piece of candy, 1 oz. of juice in a small cup, or tickles for 5 seconds. If your child takes the item (e.g., eats the candy) or appears to enjoy it (e.g., laughs when tickled), you can start teaching. If not, you will have to introduce another item until you find something that is appealing.

After your child has accessed the item or activity one time, present it again. This time, prompt, or help, your child to make a hand sign to request it. There are two ways to prompt. The first way is to model or show the sign to your child by performing it yourself. *Modeling* is most appropriate for children who are able to imitate others' movements. The second way is to place your hands over your child's hands and physically mold the sign for him or her. This type of prompting is more appropriate for children who cannot imitate. After you have prompted your child to make the sign, give him or her immediate (i.e., in less than 1 second) access to the item. Repeat these steps. Try to delay your prompt for a few seconds to see if your child will make the sign on his or her own. Some children may require numerous prompts to learn a sign; others may require fewer prompts.

If you are teaching only one sign, your child may quickly grow bored. If so, give him or her short breaks by allowing access to different items or activities. If you are teaching more than one sign, alternating between signs also will decrease the likelihood of boredom.

ARRANGING OTHER OPPORTUNITIES TO COMMUNICATE

Your child probably will get the urge to request an item or activity at other times during the day. Once he or she has learned one sign, try to arrange opportunities for him or her to use the sign outside of the training setting. You might do this by placing a preferred item in view but out of reach. For example, place preferred cookies in a transparent container on a shelf in the kitchen. When your child approaches the cookies, prompt him or her to make the sign. Each child may need a different number of learning opportunities before he or she begins to use signs spontaneously. Some children may require dozens of learning opportunities every day before they use signs on their own.

SUMMARY

Sign language training can be an effective way to teach children with autism to communicate. Some children may develop a vocabulary of only one or two signs, while others may learn considerably more. Start sign language training by teaching your child to request a preferred item or activity. You will increase your child's likelihood of success by arranging a number of opportunities for him or her to use signs throughout the day.

PRINT RESOURCE

Sundberg, M. L., & Partington, J. W. (1998). *Teaching language to children with autism and other developmental disabilities.* Danville, CA: Behavior Analysts.

KEY TERMS

AUGMENTATIVE AND ALTERNATIVE COMMUNICATION (AAC): Any communication that uses something other than speech

SEE ALSO THESE RELATED ENTRIES:

ASSISTIVE TECHNOLOGY AND AUTISM

E. Amanda Boutot, Matt Tincani, and Yvonne Randall

BECAUSE many people with autism have difficulty in communicating, finding other ways to express their wants and needs is crucial for them to function independently in society. The use of assistive technology (AT) has helped to improve the abilities of people with autism, particularly in the area of communication. Although many devices are available, families need to know about the effectiveness of each device so that they can help make the best possible AT choice for their child. The types of devices and issues in making AT decisions are discussed in this entry, but we also urge parents to contact the AT department of their local school system or a community agency that specializes in AT equipment (e.g., United Cerebral Palsy).

TYPES OF DEVICES

Various devices are available for children with autism, including picture-cued schedules, alternative communication devices, video equipment, and computer programs. AT devices range from low tech to high tech, with varying degrees of availability.

Picture-cued schedules often are used to help a child with autism identify tasks within the daily routine through clip art or actual photographs of the task. Allowing children to choose among visual symbols improves their ability to communicate with other children and adults without the requirement of language recall skills. Such schedule systems are relatively inexpensive and easy to create. They can be modified to each individual child's specific needs, as well as to the environment in which they will be used; for example, at home the schedule system may hang on the pantry door or in your child's room. Some families create systems in folders or on clipboards that can be carried on family outings. The systems can be large or small, depending on your child's needs and space availability. As new or different activities are added to the daily routine, replacement or new pictures can be obtained via computer or photographs you take. The use of schedule systems is widely cited as a best practice in the field of autism.

The *Picture Exchange Communication System* (PECS; Frost & Bondy, 2002) is the most widely used picture-based alternative communication system for children with autism. PECS is an instructional system for teaching a child who does not speak to approach a person and offer him or her a picture symbol to make a need or want known. The PECS system is unique because it breaks down the teaching process into discrete phases, beginning with the basic picture exchange and progressing to the formation of sentences. Although PECS is very popular and effective for many children with autism, you do not need to use this method exclusively. We encourage families and teachers to find the system or method that works best for the particular child. The goal is to give your child an alternative way to communicate when speech is not an option.

A promising area for teaching developmental skills, such as self-help skills, is through *videotapes*. The ability to replay a videotape provides the repetition many young children require to master a particular skill. You or your child's teachers can videotape your child (or a sibling or peer) performing a task and use this tape to help your child with autism see what he or she should be doing.

Some children with autism require more sophisticated, high-tech systems. In these cases, upgraded computer hardware and software applications often are the first areas explored. Other applications, such as voice-output communication aids (VOCAs), may be required for the child with language delays to be able to interact with his or her peers.

DECIDING ON AT EQUIPMENT

When deciding on the type of AT devices to be used by your child, school staff members need to consider the home environment, as well as that of the school. Conducting an ecological assessment in the home and community where your child most likely will use the device will allow the team (including you and school personnel) to make an equipment decision that is appropriate for all environments in which your child will use the device. Problems often arise when equipment that is appropriate for use at school is not functional in the home or community. For example, if the primary language spoken in the home is not English, the device needs to include output in both English and the home language. The family therefore must participate in the assessment and in a meeting to determine the type of device and how and when it will be used with their child. If parents are not informed, it most likely will be impossible for them to use the device at home. Any communication program must be appropriate for your child to use in all environments.

Another issue that families need to be aware is the availability of the device at home. Ask the school staff members if they will come to your home and demonstrate its use. Also, ask what the policies are for checking out the device to take home in the evenings, on weekends, and during holiday breaks (including summer vacations). Many high-tech devices are very expensive and require specialized training, so these are issues that may make a difference in the decision to use them. Above all, parents must feel comfortable that the AT device chosen for their child is appropriate, effective, and user friendly not just for the child with autism but for the whole family.

REFERENCE

Frost, L., & Bondy, A. (2002). *Picture exchange communication system*. Newark, DE: Pyramid Educational Products.

PRINT RESOURCES

Lindsay, J. D. (Ed.). (2000). *Technology and exceptional individuals* (3rd ed.). Austin, TX: PRO-ED.

Lord, C., & McGee, J. P. (Eds.). (2001). *Educating children with autism*. Washington, DC: National Academy Press.

Quill, K. A. (1997). Instructional considerations for young children with autism: The rationale for visually cued instruction. *Journal of Autism and Developmental Disorders, 27*, 697–714.

Scheuermann, B., & Webber, J. (2002). *Autism: Teaching does make a difference*. Belmont, CA: Wadsworth.

Technology-Related Assistance for Individuals with Disabilities Act of 1988, 29 U.S.C. § 2201 *et seq.*

WEB RESOURCES

ABLEDATA (http://www.abledata.com)

The Autism Society of America (http://www.autism-society.org)

United Cerebral Palsy (http://www.ucp.org)

KEY TERMS

ASSISTIVE TECHNOLOGY: Any device, either low tech or high tech, that assists a person with a disability to function more independently in his or her daily life

HIGH-TECH DEVICES: Devices that require batteries or electricity to run, such as computers or voice-output devices

LOW-TECH DEVICES: Devices that are relatively inexpensive and easy to create, such as picture schedules or foam grips to aid in holding a pencil or toothbrush

PICTURE EXCHANGE COMMUNICATION SYSTEM (PECS): An AAC system using picture symbols

VOICE-OUTPUT DEVICES: When a certain button or switch is pushed or activated, these devices will speak for a person with a disability

SEE ALSO THESE RELATED ENTRIES:

FACILITATED COMMUNICATION

Laura Lacey Rismiller

THIS entry deals with an intervention called *facilitated communication* (FC) that some school personnel or therapists may recommend if your child is nonverbal (e.g., autistic, has a developmental disability). Although this procedure may still be employed as a communication intervention, the scientific community largely has discredited it. This entry relates the history of FC, gives an overview of what the research has to say, and gives advice to parents seeking more information.

WHAT IS FACILITATED COMMUNICATION?

FC is a procedure in which a person (facilitator) uses some degree of physical assistance to help a nonverbal individual with autism or some other developmental disability spell out messages by touching letters on a display.

The facilitator typically supports the hand of the individual as he or she uses his or her index finger to point to specific letters on a letter board or to touch individual keys on an electronic keyboard. The facilitator may be a teacher (or other professional), a paraprofessional (e.g., an aide), or a parent.

WHAT IS THE HISTORY OF FC?

FC started in the 1970s with a teacher by the name of Rosemary Crossley. She worked in an institution in Melbourne, Australia, with individuals with severe cerebral palsy. Crossley was convinced that several of her students had developed academic skills even though they had been institutionalized and given little or no education for most of their lives. She stated that her students could demonstrate these skills if they were given hand or arm support to help them point to letters or pictures.

In 1986, Crossley started the Dignity Through Education and Language Center (DEAL) in Melbourne. Her goal was to promote FC for persons with severe communication impairments. Controversy regarding the FC methods that Crossley was using and promoting immediately erupted. One reason is because Crossley was resistant to formal, objective testing. Several controlled investigations were conducted to test the efficacy of FC, however. Results from these early studies suggested that FC had little merit and was not an effective method for persons with severe communication impairments. FC made its way to the United States when, after studying with Crossley at the DEAL Center, Douglas Biklin established the FC Institute (FCI) at Syracuse University.

WHAT DOES THE RESEARCH SAY?

Researchers have conducted many studies of FC using formal, objective testing, and these studies consistently have shown that FC is *not* an effective intervention for persons with communication disorders (e.g., autism, developmental disabilities). Time after time, study results indicated that the facilitator influenced the responses of the individual to whom they were trying to lend support. For example, results showed that correct answers were given only when the facilitator knew those answers and were *never* typed when the facilitator had information that was different from what was given to the person he or she was assisting.

In 1994, the American Psychological Association adopted the position that FC is a "controversial and unproved communicative procedure with no scientifically demonstrated support for its efficacy" (p. 1).

The American Speech-Language-Hearing Association (1995) published a position statement, concluding that the "validity and reliability of Facilitated Communication has not been demonstrated to date" and that "information obtained through or based on Facilitated Communication should not form the sole basis for making any diagnostic or treatment decisions" (p. 1).

HEALTHY SKEPTICISM

Many programs and interventions are targeted at parents who believe they have exhausted all other possibilities when it comes to communicating with their child. It is critical to look at these programs objectively and without any sort of bias. Any program that makes impressive claims also should make available data that verify its effectiveness.

A PARENT'S DILEMMA

Raising and caring for a child who has autism or other developmental disabilities is extremely difficult. Parents of children who are nonverbal are especially challenged because of the barriers they face when attempting to communicate with their child. It is only natural to want your child to "talk" to you; hence, many parents will do just about anything to make communication possible.

The following are some suggestions for parents who are looking for interventions for their child with communication difficulties:

1. Know what your child's strengths and abilities are. Select a program or intervention that emphasizes those strengths.

2. Any communication that requires the use of something other than a person's own body is called *augmentative and alternative communication* (AAC). Hundreds of AAC programs and devices are available. Check out the Web site for The Alliance for Technology Access (http://www.ataccess.org) for parent support groups and information about communication evaluations and assistive technology.

3. Be sure to objectively evaluate any possible intervention by asking the following questions:
   - What does the research say about this intervention/program?
   - Has it been shown to be effective in formal, objective studies, or are the reports mainly opinions and testimonials?
   - Is it appropriate for my child? Does it fit into my child's long-term plan?

REFERENCES

American Psychological Association. (1994). *Resolution on facilitated communication by the American Psychological Association*. Adopted in Council, August 14, 1994, Los Angeles, California.

American Speech-Language-Hearing Association. (1995, March). Position statement on facilitated communication. *ASHA, 37,* 22.

PRINT RESOURCES

Green, G. (1994). Facilitated communication: Mental miracle or sleight of hand? *Skeptic, 2,* 3, 68–76.

Montee, B., Miltenberger, R. G., & Wittrock, D. (1995). An experimental analysis of facilitated communication. *Journal of Applied Behavior Analysis, 28,* 189–200.

KEY TERM

AUGMENTATIVE AND ALTERNATIVE COMMUNICATION **(AAC):** Any communication system that uses something other than speech

SEE ALSO THESE RELATED ENTRIES:

HYPERLEXIA

Marc Tedoff

THE American Hyperlexia Association (n.d.) defines *hyperlexia* as an ability to read that is far above what is typical for the child's age or an intense fascination with letters or numbers. This entry discusses strategies for teaching functional communication skills to children with hyperlexia.

STRATEGIES FOR TEACHING A CHILD WHO IS HYPERLEXIC

When a child is hyperlexic, he or she can read words well beyond what would be expected. Therefore, what is most important is how to most effectively capitalize on his or her hyperlexia.

SCRIPTING

Using the reading skills of children who display hyperlexic abilities to teach them language and new skills can be effective. One of the teaching techniques you might use is teaching communication and social skills through *scripts* for various situations. Scripts can be taught for going to the park, playing with friends, going to the restaurant, greeting new people, and other social situations in which your child will be involved. Scripts can be developed by listening to and writing down or taping what typically developing children do and say as they communicate in various settings. One way to do scripting is to use a Bell & Howell Language Master. This is a machine that accepts index cards with a magnetic strip on the bottom. Blank cards can be purchased and used to record half of a script. Each card should be numbered, and the script can be written on the card for the child to see and read as he or she listens. The visual and audio script then can be gradually used less and less as your child begins to memorize his or her lines. Your child also should be introduced to a same-age child without disabilities who has been taught the other half of the script. Cards can be purchased with preprinted and prerecorded common objects (e.g., animals, furniture, transportation); these cards are useful for expanding your child's vocabulary.

PROMPTING

Another teaching strategy uses *written prompts.* Kistner, Robbins, and Haskett (1988) reported on a very successful intervention that taught children with hyperlexia how to make a request by using written prompts. Kistner et al. gave the child in their study a prompt card that had on it *want cookie.* Once the child memorized the prompt, it was presented to the child during a snack time with a cookie. The written prompt was quickly cut back, and the requesting behavior continued. The researchers also expanded on this skill by presenting prompt cards and various items in different settings (e.g., milk and a prompt card for *want* was presented to the child in the kitchen).

PROVIDING CHOICES

Communicating in *concrete terms* is important. For example, don't ask, "What do you want to eat?" Instead, provide two choices. You should allow for pauses in interactions so your child can have some time to understand what is happening.

TURN TAKING

Develop *turn-taking skills* through games that later can be translated to *communicative reciprocity*, which also can be taught in rote through scripting. Start by teaching one exchange based on concrete concepts. For example, give your child a toy car. While holding a toy truck, say, "I have a truck," and then prompt your child (using written cues, if necessary) to respond, "I have a car." Once your child has memorized this exchange, change the props you use so your child can learn to use the skill with other items. Use an object your child is already familiar with to reduce confusion. Once this simple exchange is mastered, introduce another exchange. For example, after the initial exchange say, "My truck is blue," and teach your child to respond in kind, "My car is red."

Another strategy to encourage language development is combining rote phrases your child has learned to expand language usage and sentence length. A child who has learned to say, "My name is Billy," in response to the question "What is your name?" and also has learned to respond, "Good, how are you?" in response to the greeting, "How are you?" can be encouraged to combine these two phrases when meeting a new person: "My name is Billy. How are you?"

TEACHING YES AND NO

Teach *yes* and *no* in isolation for preferred and nonpreferred items, in relation to objects and in relation to concepts. To teach preferred and nonpreferred, use your child's favorite food and a mixture that no one would eat (e.g., pickles and ice cream). Offer each food to your child and teach him or her to respond appropriately to the offer, using written prompts as necessary. Teach *yes* and *no* in relation to objects by offering familiar objects to your child and asking, "Is this a (object name)?" Teaching *yes* and *no* in relation to concepts is a little different because there are many different concepts to consider. For example, it is different to ask, "Do you want to go out to dinner?" than it is to ask, "Do you see an elephant?" Teaching appropriate responses to these types of questions is the same, however. The answers again should be taught in rote and generalized as quickly as possible.

Teach the answers to "what, where, when, and why" questions, the functions of objects and community helpers, and the answers to social questions in rote. Use written prompts and the Language Master if necessary. Before you actually use a prompt, you should have a plan to lessen use of that prompt (*fading*) as soon as possible; otherwise, you risk having your child become dependent on the prompt. Written prompts can be faded letter by letter or by slowly masking them until they are no longer visible. Verbal prompts can be faded by changing your tone of voice or length of utterance (do not say the whole word).

SUMMARY

It may be true that more work is involved in teaching our children with hyperlexia, but the investment in time and effort is absolutely worth it. Two excellent resources are available to help you in your efforts. The first is the American Hyperlexia Association. Its Web site is full of practical, hands-on information and provides a wealth of other resources to pursue. The second is the Center for Speech and Language Disorders. The center also has a Web site and provides very useful, practical information and other resources.

REFERENCES

American Hyperlexia Association (n.d.). Retrieved September 4, 2008, from http://www.hyperlexia.org.

Kistner, J., Robbins, F., & Haskett, M. (1988). Assessment and skill remediation of hyperlexic children. *Journal of Autism and Developmental Disorders, 18*, 191–205.

PRINT RESOURCE

Fisher, W., Burd, L., & Kerbeshian, J. (1988). Markers for improvement in children with pervasive developmental disorders. *Journal of Mental Deficiency Research, 32*, 357–369.

WEB RESOURCE

American Hyperlexia Association (http://www.hyperlexia.org)

Center for Speech and Language Disorders (http://www.csld.com)

KEY TERMS

PROMPTING: Providing cues, such as a verbal hint or a written reminder

SCRIPTING: Providing a written or verbal script for a child to follow in a certain situations, usually social ones, to promote success

SECTION
5

ISSUES IN
BEHAVIOR

WORKING WITH STRENGTHS

E. Amanda Boutot

PARENTS and teachers know that children with autism may have some limitations in the areas of language or social skills but that these children also have strengths. Particular strengths shared by many children with autism are memory and an ability to follow a structured routine. In fact, many children with autism *insist* on having things the same way time after time, day after day, and learn routines very quickly. When things do not go as expected, parents and teachers often are faced with challenging behaviors and expressions of frustration. To increase the success of children with autism and decrease their challenging behaviors, this entry offers strategies for working with their strengths.

STICKING TO ROUTINES

RECOGNIZE YOUR CHILD'S NEED FOR FAMILIARITY

Young children like repetition. For example, they like the predictability of familiar stories or songs and may ask their parents to read the same story or sing the same song over and over again. This makes sense: When you are very young, you do not yet have the experience or cognitive ability to understand all that is going on in the world around you. In fact, your world may feel somewhat chaotic, given your limited knowledge base and emerging language skills. At any age, people with autism may face similar challenges as they try to make sense out of a seemingly chaotic world and find peace and comfort in familiar things. For this reason, having a typical household or daily routine can make an important difference for a child with autism.

HELP TO MAKE SENSE OUT OF CHAOS

Busy families may find it difficult to set up a routine that they can stick with day in and day out. You may find, however, that you are more regimented than you thought. Spend a few days just keeping track of what you do each day. Put a sheet of paper on the refrigerator with the times of the day broken down into 30-minute or hour segments, starting with the typical waking time of the earliest riser to the latest bedtime. Have each family member mark his or her activities in the correct time slot, perhaps using a different color pen or a special symbol for each person. Examine the lists to see if you can find an emerging typical routine for your family. You may find that you can adapt some activities to create a more typical routine. Once you have settled on what a typical day or week looks like for your family, write it out and post it for everyone to see. All family members will have a better understanding of what everyone else is up to, as well as a reminder that routine is an important part of helping the person with autism be successful in his or her daily life. It is important to emphasize that a consistent routine is crucial to this success.

INSISTENCE ON SAMENESS

TRY TO KEEP THINGS PREDICTABLE

Your family needs to do things in as similar a way as possible each day. For example, if you always use the downstairs bathroom for brushing teeth, your child with autism may feel uncomfortable when you try to brush his or her teeth upstairs. Although it is not always practical, when possible, families should try to do things in a similar manner each time to relieve some of the stress and anxiety the child with autism feels because of changes. When changes are going to occur (e.g., company is coming, so your child cannot sit in his or her usual chair, or the blue cup is in the dishwasher) you need to realize that this may cause your child some discomfort and be prepared with alternatives. For example, use simple language or picture cues to let your child know that something different is going to happen. If your child has a favorite video, but the family wishes to watch the World Series, for instance, allow your child to watch her or his video for a short period of time (e.g., 5 minutes). Using a timer to signal the end of video time, turn the television and guide your child toward another desired activity. Once your child has encountered the change in routine, be sure to reward him or her with an activity or item he or she likes and provide praise for appropriately accepting change.

INTRODUCE CHANGES GRADUALLY

Families rarely have a set routine that is followed each and every day, and even if you are fortunate enough to be able to make this happen in your house, it may not be the most appropriate choice for your child. In real life, change happens. Children with autism need to come to an understanding and acceptance of this, just as we all do. Therefore, you will want to set your child up for success from the beginning. Once your child has begun to get accustomed to the way things are done, begin to introduce changes slowly and gradually so that he or she can begin to learn to accept that things cannot always be exactly the same each time. For example, after taking the same route to the grocery store, introduce changes in the route slowly. Begin with small steps by first parking on a different side of the lot than usual, and then begin entering the parking lot from a different entrance. Next, go around the block and enter from a different street. This way, your child learns that even though it is not the exact same approach, you always end up in the same location.

SUMMARY

The world can be a chaotic place for young children, especially for many children with autism, due to their lack of experience or limited ability to understand those around them. Like all young children, children with autism thrive on routine and often insist on things being done the same way over and over again, becoming frustrated when changes occur. This ability to recognize routine is one of your child's many strengths. You can use this strength to make your child's world seem less chaotic and to gradually teach acceptance of change. Once children expect certain routines, they begin to need less adult direction and can start to do things independently. This is an important goal for any child, but especially for a child with autism.

PRINT RESOURCES

Quill, K. A. (1995). *Teaching children with autism: Strategies to enhance communication and socialization*. New York: Delmar.

Scheuermann, B., & Webber, J. (2002). *Autism: Teaching does make a difference*. Belmont, CA: Wadsworth.

Simpson, R. L., & Regan, M. (1988). *Management of autistic behavior*. Austin, TX: PRO-ED.

KEY TERMS

CHALLENGING BEHAVIORS: Inappropriate behaviors often seen when children with autism are frustrated

CHANGE: Any alteration to a routine or activity that is different from what is expected

ROUTINE: The way things are usually done or expected

SEE ALSO THESE RELATED ENTRIES:

DEVELOPING SCHEDULES FOR IMPROVED BEHAVIOR AND INDEPENDENCE

E. Amanda Boutot

CHILDREN with autism have a unique gift: the ability to adhere to routines and an intense desire for sameness. Although any parent who has witnessed a "meltdown" due to a slight change in routine may question whether this is indeed a positive trait, the fact is that parents can work with this desire for routine and sameness to improve their child's independence and decrease these meltdowns. One way to do this is through the use of schedule systems, sometimes referred to as *calendars*, which provide visual cues about the day's activities. This entry discusses guidelines for and types of schedules, how to create a schedule for your child, and methods for teaching your child how to use it.

A visual activity schedule acts much the same way as a grocery list or a checklist that adults may keep to help them organize their time. The goals are to choose a schedule system that the child understands and to teach him or her to follow it independently.

GUIDELINES FOR SCHEDULES

To be most effective, schedules must be visual, they must be in a format (type) that the child understands, they must include all activities in the child's day, they must be displayed in a readable format, and they must include a method for designating that an activity has been completed. Deciding on the type of schedule and what to include are addressed later in this entry. To ensure a readable format, have the schedule displayed either left to right or top to bottom. A top-to-bottom arrangement is best when there is limited space in which to display all of the activities; a left-to-right schedule is good because it follows the same format as reading. To show that an activity has been completed, include a "Finished" box or envelope, a means of checking off items on a list, or a way to move items from one side of the schedule to the other. A visual representation that an activity has been completed is key to helping your child understand the system.

TYPES OF SCHEDULES

There are three types of schedules that parents may create, depending on their child's level of functioning. These are listed next.

SCHEDULES USING WRITTEN WORDS

For children who can read, a written list is an appropriate type of schedule. These lists simply may be the names of the activities (e.g., "dressing") or a description of what is to be done during an activity (e.g., "put on shirt, pants, socks, and shoes"). It is best to use words that your child already can read, although teaching new words may be necessary. Your child should be encouraged to read his or her list, although another family member also may read the list aloud. Some families create lists with boxes out to the side of each item in which a check mark or an "X" can show that the item has been completed. Other families will print the words on individual index cards or strips of paper that can be moved to a "Finished" envelope or box or to the other side of the schedule. Families also may choose to color-code activities according to everyday events (e.g., meals) and special occasions, such as going to the park or a movie.

SCHEDULES USING PICTURES

For children who are not yet reading on their own but who are able to recognize objects in photographs, picture schedules are recommended. Parents can take photos of everyday and special activities in which their child might be involved and put them on laminated index cards. You may want to write the name of each activity under the picture on the cards so that your child can begin to recognize sight words related to everyday activities (and so that he or she can later move to a written schedule). Pictures of your child engaged in a particular activity (e.g., brushing his or her teeth) or of the items related to that activity (e.g., toothbrush, toothpaste) are good choices. An alternative to photographs, which may have distracting colors or objects in them that prevent a child from learning to distinguish one from the other, is line drawings. These line drawings are available commercially from any of the companies listed at the end of this entry. Your child's teacher also may have line drawings that can be copied and used by your family.

SCHEDULES USING OBJECTS

Some children with autism have difficulty recognizing items in two-dimensional photographs and therefore need three-dimensional objects. These objects may be actual size (e.g., a spoon for eating), or miniature (e.g., a toy bus to indicate when to go to school). The objects should have some relevance to the activity (e.g., a stick for playing outside) but may be symbolic (e.g., a piece of fabric for naptime, a special toy for riding in the car). The key is that the symbol used to represent each activity remains the same so that your child learns to associate each symbol with its corresponding activity.

CREATING YOUR CHILD'S SCHEDULE

Several steps are involved in creating a schedule system. You will want to first decide which type of schedule will work best for your child before you create it. The second step is to decide which daily activities will be put on the schedule. Due to limited space, it may not be possible to have every activity on the schedule; you will want to choose those activities that your child has the most difficulty doing or that he or she does not do independently and start with them. You also might be able to create one system for the mornings and another one for the afternoons or repost items for the afternoon, after morning activities have been completed. Spend a few days or a week writing down what your child does each day; this will help you to identify all possible activities. Third, you will need to decide how and where to post the schedule. Have a system that is clearly visible in a common area of the house, although if you are using written words, you may find that having a list on a clipboard or in a binder that your child can carry throughout the day works best. Space also is often an issue. Try to find an area on a wall that your child can reach easily. Often schedules are placed on poster boards or large pieces of cardboard. The size of the system will depend on the space you have available. For three-dimensional objects, small boxes on a low table are recommended. The fourth step is to create the system. This includes making the list of written words, making picture or line drawing cards, or finding three-dimensional objects for each activity. Attaching the photo or line drawing cards to a board with an adhesive-like Velcro allows the items to be removed. You also will need to create the "Finished" box or envelope and label it as such. The final step is teaching the system to your child.

TEACHING YOUR CHILD THE SYSTEM

The key to successfully teaching your child to use the schedule system is to be consistent: Use it every day. You may need to start by showing your child how to use it or by giving him or her hand-over-hand assistance to pick up cards or objects. You may want your child to carry the card or object with him or her to the area where the activity will occur (e.g., taking the spoon to the table for a snack), or you may have him or her only look at it on the board. Do not forget to have your child put the item in the "Finished" box or envelope, check the item off, or move it from one side of the board to the other when the activity is completed.

SUMMARY

Most children with autism prefer routine and consistency to change. Very often, these children lack the receptive language skills to fully understand when someone tells them that there will be a change; thus, they may display inappropriate behaviors (e.g., tantrums) when a change does occur. According to Scheuermann and Webber (2002), providing children with schedules that visually display daily activities helps them better understand expectations, make predictions about events, anticipate changes, make choices, and operate independently.

REFERENCE

Scheuermann, B., & Webber, J. A. (2002). *Autism: Teaching does make a difference*. Belmont, CA: Wadsworth.

WEB RESOURCES

Boardmaker (http://www.mayer-johnson.com)

Pyramid Educational Consultants (http://www.pecs.com)

KEY TERMS

HAND-OVER-HAND PROMPTING: A method of showing the child how to do something, for example, using hand-over-hand assistance to pick up a card or object

LINE DRAWINGS: Simple drawings that do not contain distracting colors or objects in them that would prevent a child from learning to distinguish one from the other; available commercially from many companies; the child's teacher will have some that can be duplicated

SIGHT WORDS: Photos of everyday and special activities with the name of each activity written under the picture so the child will begin to recognize the word

TRANSITION: Moving from one event or activity to another

SEE ALSO THESE RELATED ENTRIES:

FUNCTIONAL BEHAVIORAL ASSESSMENT

Matt Tincani

WHAT IS FUNCTIONAL BEHAVIORAL ASSESSMENT?

Functional behavioral assessment (FBA; sometimes called *functional assessment*) is the process of identifying situations that produce challenging behavior. You may have heard about FBA in regard to your child's educational program. If your child exhibits challenging behavior, her or his educational team should conduct an FBA as a first step toward reducing or eliminating the behavior. Under the 1997 amendments to the Individuals with Disabilities Education Act, children who exhibit challenging behavior must receive an FBA, and the results must be incorporated into a behavioral intervention program (BIP).

WHY DOES MY CHILD EXHIBIT CHALLENGING BEHAVIOR?

There are many reasons why children with autism exhibit challenging behaviors. Like all children, they sometimes have "bad days." Sleep deprivation, disruptions to their routine, difficult academic assignments, and other unpleasant events can trigger challenging behavior episodes. Because children with autism often have limited communication skills, they also may learn to use a challenging behavior to produce a desired outcome. For example, if your child is given a difficult task that he or she does not understand, he or she may pinch, hit, or scream to escape from it. FBA is the process for identifying these types of situations that produce challenging behavior. When the educational team understands what they are, the team can design a BIP to reduce or eliminate them. Three categories of variables control challenging behavior: setting events, antecedents, and consequences.

SETTING EVENTS

Setting events change the momentary value of reinforcers associated with challenging behavior. For example, if your child has not had a drink all morning (setting event), liquid becomes momentarily reinforcing. Behaviors associated with obtaining the liquid (e.g., asking for a drink, visiting the water fountain) are now more likely. If your child engages in challenging behavior to get liquids (e.g., hitting, biting), these behaviors are more likely. Similarly, if your child slept fewer than 5 hours the night before (setting event), escape from an assignment may become momentarily reinforcing. If presented with an assignment he or she does not like, your child is more likely to pinch or hit to help her or him escape from the assignment. Common examples of setting events for children with autism include sleep deprivation, disruptions to medication routines, disruptions to daily schedules, and periods of nonengagement, which increase the value of reinforcers associated with challenging behavior.

ANTECEDENTS

Antecedents trigger challenging behavior. Often, antecedents involve the presentation of unpleasant tasks, unfamiliar situations, or nonpreferred people, known as *aversive stimuli.* In the presence of these stimuli, your child will engage in challenging behavior to escape or avoid them. For example, the teacher gives your child a difficult assignment and he or she screams so that he or she will be given a break. Antecedents also involve the presentation of preferred stimuli, such as food and drink, activities, and people your child likes. In the presence of these stimuli, your child will engage in challenging behavior to obtain them. For example, a teacher places a pitcher of juice on the table and your child screams so that the teacher will pour him or her a cup.

CONSEQUENCES

Consequences reinforce challenging behavior. If the challenging behavior produces a desired event, the consequence is *positive reinforcement.* An example would be when your child hits to get the attention of a peer or screams to get a favorite toy. The consequence is *negative reinforcement* if the challenging behavior removes an undesired event. An example would be when your child destroys work materials to escape from a disliked assignment.

The diagrams in Figure 3 illustrate how setting events, antecedents, and consequences work to produce challenging behavior.

When considering what a behavior does, keep in mind that well-intended intervention procedures actually can strengthen an undesirable behavior. In the first diagram in Figure 3, the time-out procedure is reinforcing hitting and screaming because it allows the child to escape from the difficult assignment. To avoid

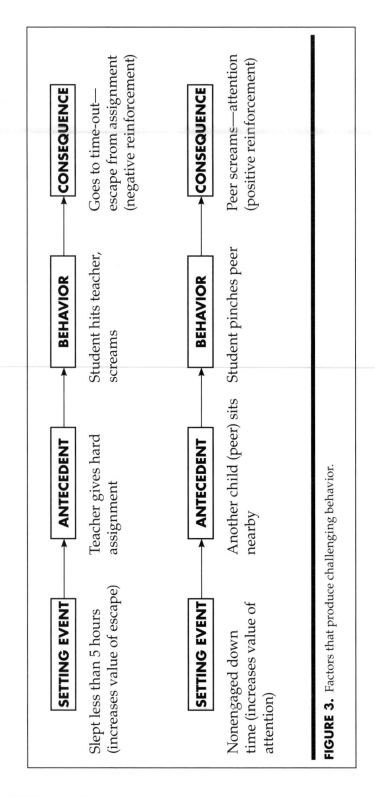

FIGURE 3. Factors that produce challenging behavior.

inadvertently triggering or reinforcing challenging behavior, FBA must be used as the basis for the BIP.

HOW TO CONDUCT AN FBA

Many methods for conducting FBA are available. They can be categorized into three types: *indirect assessment, direct assessment,* and *functional analysis* (Heron & Harris, 2001). The potential advantages and disadvantages of each are described.

INDIRECT ASSESSMENT

This involves interviewing persons, such as teachers, who have access to your child. In an informal indirect assessment, the interviewer asks unstructured questions to identify functions. Because it is subjective, I do not recommend using informal indirect assessment unless the interviewer has considerable skill and experience in conducting FBA. In formal indirect assessment, the interviewer uses a structured questionnaire to identify functions. Examples include the *Functional Assessment Interview Form* and *Parent Directed Functional Assessment* (O'Neill et al., 1997) and the *Motivational Assessment Scale* (Durand & Crimmins, 1988). Formal assessments consist of specific interview questions that attempt to identify the setting events, antecedents, and consequences associated with challenging behavior. Indirect assessments have the advantage of being convenient and relatively easy to use, but they may be less accurate.

DIRECT ASSESSMENT

This involves observation of your child at home, in the classroom, or in community settings. Direct assessment can be more reliable than indirect assessment because your child is observed in settings where the challenging behavior actually occurs. Direct assessment often involves recording what happened before the behavior (i.e., antecedents), the behavior itself, and what occurred after the behavior (i.e., consequences). Examples of direct functional assessment include the ABC assessment (Bijou, Peterson, & Ault, 1968), scatter plot assessment (Touchette, MacDonald, & Langer, 1985), and the *Functional Assessment Observation Form* (O'Neill et al., 1997). Figure 4 is an example of an ABC assessment with hypothetical data.

The observer notes the time the challenging behavior occurred, what happened just before the behavior, and what happened just after the behavior. He or she will look for patterns of antecedents and consequences over time to establish how the behavior functions. For example, if after several days of observation the professional notes that sitting alone and transition consistently precede aggression, these probably are triggers. Similarly, if being redirected by the teacher is a consistent consequence for aggression, it is probably reinforcing that aggression.

Direct assessment often requires more time and effort than indirect assessment. In addition, it is less likely to identify setting events that may precede the challenging behavior by several hours or more.

FUNCTIONAL ANALYSIS

Functional analysis is the experimental manipulation of variables hypothesized to trigger and maintain a challenging behavior (Iwata, Dorsey, Slifer, Bauman, & Richman, 1982/1994). Rather than simply observing the student, the professional sets up situations in which the problem behavior is likely to occur. For example, if the behavior is thought to be maintained by escape from task demands, the experimenter will give the child a demand-

Student: Raymond	Observer: Ms. Muñoz	Date: 11/30
Time begin: 8:30	Time end: 3:30	

Time	Antecedent	Behavior	Consequence
8:57 a.m.	Sitting alone	Pinching	Redirected by teacher
9:31 a.m.	Transition	Hitting, yelling	Redirected by teacher
11:50 a.m.	Worksheet	Tearing	Time-out

FIGURE 4. A hypothetical ABC assessment.

ing task and will remove the task when the child performs the challenging behavior. If the behavior occurs under these circumstances, it is probably maintained by escape from task demands. Functional analysis is more time-consuming than direct and indirect assessment and should be conducted only by trained professionals.

FBA AND BEHAVIORAL INTERVENTION PLANNING

Although behavioral intervention planning is beyond the scope of this entry, keep in mind that an effective BIP must be guided by a functional assessment. Well-intentioned BIPs can inadvertently strengthen a challenging behavior if they fail to address why the behavior occurs. As your child's advocate, you should ensure that the educational team understands the functional assessment process within the context of behavioral intervention planning.

REFERENCES

Bijou, S. W., Peterson, R. F., & Ault, M. H. (1968). A method to integrate descriptive and experimental field studies at the level of data and empirical concept. *Journal of Applied Behavior Analysis, 1*, 175–191.

Durand, V. M., & Crimmins, D. B. (1988). Identifying the variables that maintain self-injurious behavior. *Journal of Autism and Developmental Disabilities, 18*, 99–117.

Heron, T. E., & Harris, K. (2001). *The educational consultant: Helping professionals, parents, and students in inclusive classrooms* (4th ed.). Austin, TX: PRO-ED.

Iwata, B. A., Dorsey, M., Slifer, K., Bauman, K., & Richman, G. (1982/1994). Towards a functional analysis of self-injury. *Analysis and Intervention in Developmental Disabilities, 2*, 3–20. (Reprinted in *Journal of Applied Behavior Analysis, 27*, 197–209)

O'Neill, R. E., Horner, R. H., Albin, R. W., Sprague, J., Storey, K., & Newton, J. S. (1997). *Functional assessment and program development for problem behavior: A practical handbook*. Pacific Grove, CA: Brooks/Cole.

Touchette, P. E., MacDonald, R. F., & Langer, S. N. (1985). A scatter plot for identifying stimulus control of challenging behavior. *Journal of Applied Behavior Analysis, 18*, 343–351.

KEY TERMS

ANTECEDENTS: Events that trigger challenging behavior; these can involve the presentation of aversive stimuli, such as unpleasant tasks and nonpreferred people

CONSEQUENCES: Events that reinforce challenging behavior: If the challenging behavior produces a desired event, the consequence is positive reinforcement; if the challenging behavior removes an undesired event, the consequence is negative reinforcement

DIRECT ASSESSMENT: Involves observation of the student in home, classroom, or community settings; more reliable than indirect assessment

FUNCTIONAL ANALYSIS: The experimental manipulation of variables hypothesized to occasion and maintain the challenging behavior; the professional sets up situations in which the problem behavior is likely to occur

FUNCTIONAL BEHAVIORAL ASSESSMENT (FBA): The process of identifying variables that produce challenging behavior; IDEA requires that children with challenging behavior receive an FBA and that the results be included in the behavior intervention program (BIP)

INDIRECT ASSESSMENT: Involves interviewing persons who have access to the child, such as parents or teachers

SETTING EVENTS: These are events that change the momentary value of reinforcers associated with challenging behavior; common examples for children with autism include sleep deprivation, disruptions to medical routines, disruptions in the daily schedule, and periods of nonengagement

SEE ALSO THESE RELATED ENTRIES:

THE POWER OF POSITIVE REINFORCEMENT

E. Amanda Boutot

IN terms of managing behavior, there really are three choices: ignore an inappropriate behavior, punish an inappropriate behavior, or reward an appropriate behavior. Ignoring behavior is not always an option, nor is it effective for many children; therefore, most parents and teachers use punishment, positive reinforcement (rewards), or a combination of both. This entry provides some truths about punishment and positive reinforcement that can help you as parents determine the most effective way to deal with your child's behaviors. Examples of positive reinforcement and guidelines for use also are included.

THE TRUTH ABOUT PUNISHMENT

By definition, *punishment* is a consequence that decreases a behavior, so it makes sense that if you want an inappropriate behavior to stop, you punish your child for doing it. However, punishment only teaches a child what *not* to do, without addressing what to do instead. One reason that parents and teachers use punishment so frequently is that it actually works very quickly to reduce an inappropriate behavior. Consider the example of a child who repeatedly is told not to touch a hot stove. When the child finally does touch it and is burned, this is a punishment and usually teaches the child very quickly that he or she should not touch the stove.

All people, including children, typically do things for a reason; in other words, there is a purpose behind all behaviors. This is true for children with autism as well. Although the purpose of some behaviors may be self-stimulatory, inappropriate behaviors often serve the purpose of communicating a want or need, particularly for children who have not developed speech or who do not have an alternative form of communication. Thus, if the inappropriate behavior is serving a useful purpose for the child, and all the adult does is punish the child, the child has no alternative way to serve his or her purpose.

One of the goals of teaching is for our children to learn skills that they can use over time and in a variety of real-world settings. In education, this is referred to as *maintenance* and *generalization*. Another truth about punishment is that it is neither maintained, nor does it generalize well. In other words, although the child may learn what not to do through punishment, this learning does not last very long, nor does it transfer to other similar situations or persons. In the example of the child who touches the hot stove, he or she learned quickly not to touch it because it burned. However, over time the child may forget this and once again touch the stove. He or she also may not understand that all stoves are potentially hot and may touch a stove in another house. Because the punishment (burning) may not occur all of the time or in other homes (because the stove is not always on and hot), the child may soon learn that it is OK to touch it again. Punishment therefore may not be the best way to teach your child skills that are to be maintained over time, in different places, and with different people.

A final truth about punishment is that although it is easy to do, it may not send the right message. The first thing that parents and teachers often think to do when a child misbehaves is punish him or her, but this leads only to increased frustration and fatigue because the punishment must be repeated. Sometimes when adults punish, they do so when they are angry. In this way, children may not associate what they have done wrong with the adult's use of punishment; they instead may see the cause of the punishment as the adult's anger. When this happens, children may become angry with the adult who imposes the punishment, rather than focusing on what they did to deserve it. This also sends the message that it is not the behavior that caused the punishment to be given but the adult's anger.

THE TRUTH ABOUT POSITIVE REINFORCEMENT

Positive reinforcement is another term for reward. By definition, reinforcement is a consequence that maintains or increases a behavior. If you want to teach your child the appropriate thing to do, you must use reinforcement. Positive reinforcement, in contrast with punishment, typically takes a bit longer to work. Given that all behavior serves a purpose, the inappropriate behavior may be highly motivating, so that even positive reinforcement is not as useful or motivating as the inappropriate behavior is for your child. Be sure to choose rewards that are more motivating than the inappropriate behavior and that serve the same purpose as the behavior.

The good news about positive reinforcement is that once it begins to work, most children are better able to maintain and generalize it than they are with punishment. Also, positive reinforcement teaches alternative behaviors, and once your child sees that these lead to the same purpose, he or she is able to see value in these behaviors and will not require rewards on a constant basis.

Finally, positive reinforcement is, by nature, more affirmative than punishment; there is little danger of your child becoming angry with you for giving him or her a reward for an appropriate behavior. Also, it is unlikely that your child will see the reward as based on your emotional state; he or she is much more likely to see that her or his actions led to the reward.

EXAMPLES OF POSITIVE REINFORCEMENT

Parents typically use three types of positive reinforcement: social rewards, tangible rewards (to include edibles), and activity rewards. This section will describe each of these in more detail.

SOCIAL REWARDS

Social rewards are those that most of us deliver and receive in a natural way throughout our lives. They are things such as a smile, a hug, a pat on the back, or praise for a job well done. They are the easiest for parents to give because they can be given anywhere and at any time. Some children with autism have difficulty relating to others, however, so a social reward often must be paired with something more tangible until these children begin to associate the tangible reward with the praise, pat on the back, and so forth.

TANGIBLE REWARDS

Tangible rewards are anything that you can give to your child, such as a sticker, a token, a star drawn or stamped on a piece of paper, a toy, or a favorite object. Edible rewards also are used, particularly for very young children or children who have no interest in any particular tangible reward. Almost all children are motivated by food (e.g., pretzels, candy, toast), even if they have limited receptive language skills with which to understand the reason they are being given the food. For children for whom other forms of positive reinforcement are not working, food rewards paired with social or tangible rewards often work best.

One way to use a tangible reward is to have it count toward another, more motivating reward. Consider, for example, a child whose favorite thing is a doll, and she is highly motivated by being able to go to the store and pick out a new doll. Her parents, however, would go broke buying a doll every time their daughter displayed an appropriate behavior. Therefore, they might instead give her stickers, a certain number of which will lead to the doll. Similarly, tangible rewards also can be used to lead to a preferred activity.

ACTIVITY REWARDS

All children have favorite activities, whether it is watching a favorite video, swimming, or engaging in self-stimulation. These preferred activities could be allowed as rewards for appropriate behavior. For example, a parent who needs his or her child to stay seated for a portion of dinner may set a timer for a set amount of time. When the timer goes off and the child has been seated the entire time, he or she can get up and go play. I recommend that parents also use a timer to indicate when the preferred activity is over. Activity rewards also may be used in combination with tangible rewards. For example, once your child has earned a certain number of stars on a card for good behavior, he or she will be allowed to play with a favorite toy.

GUIDELINES FOR POSITIVE REINFORCEMENT

No matter which positive reinforcement you choose, there are some guidelines to follow. The first is that the reward should be *immediate*. Children, especially those with autism, will not remember at the end of the day why a reward is being received. Also, when a reward is delivered immediately after an appropriate behavior has occurred, it increases the likelihood that your child is learning the appropriate behavior. Second, the reward should be *motivating*. As mentioned previously, if the reward is not as motivating or does not serve the same purpose as the inappropriate behavior, it will not work. Finally, rewards should be *eased off* (faded) as soon as your child learns the appropriate behavior or skill so that he or she does not become dependent on always having a reward for a behavior to occur. You must be careful to not fade the reinforcement too quickly, however, before the behavior has been learned.

SUMMARY

Although punishment often is the easiest and first response to an inappropriate behavior, it is not the most effective. The use of positive reinforcement not only teaches a child an alternate, more appropriate behavior; it is a kinder, gentler approach to behavior management.

PRINT RESOURCE

Scheuermann, B., & Webber, J. (2002). *Autism: Teaching does make a difference.* Belmont, CA: Wadsworth.

KEY TERMS

ACTIVITY REWARDS: Using a child's favorite activity as a reward for appropriate behavior

EDIBLE REWARDS: A food reward; used particularly for young children or children who have no interest in any particular tangible reward

GENERALIZATION: To learn skills that a child can use in a variety of real-world settings

MAINTENANCE: To learn skills that a child can use over time

PUNISHMENT: Anything that decreases a behavior; punishment only teaches a child what not to do

REINFORCEMENT/POSITIVE REINFORCEMENT: Rewards; anything that maintains or increases a behavior

SELF-STIMULATION: Repetitive, stereotyped behaviors whose sole purpose appears to be to stimulate the person's own senses

TANGIBLE REWARDS: Anything that can be given to a child, such as a sticker, a token, or a favorite object

TOKENS: Tangible rewards that can be collected to get an item or to be able to do a favorite activity

SEE ALSO THESE RELATED ENTRIES:

STRATEGIES FOR DECREASING INAPPROPRIATE BEHAVIOR

Shannon Crozier

NAPPROPRIATE behaviors are frustrating and challenging. They can be a barrier to educational, family, social, and community opportunities. Decreasing problem behaviors typically is a high priority for families. At the same time, it also is necessary to increase appropriate behaviors. Some strategies for decreasing inappropriate behavior include *punishment* and the use of *aversives.* However, there are many nonaversive, positive strategies that can achieve the same effect by making problem behavior ineffective, inefficient, and irrelevant to your child. This entry offers only a brief description of strategies. Before starting any behavior program, you should consult with a professional who is skilled in behavior management.

WHY DOES HE DO THAT AND HOW CAN I GET HIM TO STOP?

Your child's behavior serves a purpose. Even inappropriate behavior is purposeful in some way; otherwise your child would not do it. Consider the child in the grocery store who wants candy. When the parent says no, the child starts to scream. Eventually the parent gives the child the candy to stop the screaming. The child has learned that screaming is an effective way to get candy. To decrease an inappropriate behavior, you must teach your child a new, appropriate behavior so he or she can still communicate needs and wants. This entry describes some strategies for changing behavior. See Entry 8.3, Positive Behavior Supports, for additional suggestions.

REINFORCEMENT STRATEGIES

These strategies all work by reinforcing (i.e., rewarding) your child when he or she produces appropriate or desired behaviors instead of the inappropriate behavior. Reinforcing a behavior means strengthening it so it will occur more frequently. The differences among these strategies are in what you choose to strengthen. Teaching and increasing appropriate behavior can decrease unwanted, inappropriate behaviors. All of these strategies require you to keep track of your child's behavior so you can measure progress over time.

DIFFERENTIAL REINFORCEMENT OF LOWER RATES OF BEHAVIOR (DRL)

DRL is reinforcing your child for *less inappropriate behavior*. For example, your child asks for help when dressing even though he or she can get dressed independently. You can decrease the number of times your child asks for help by using rewards. First you can reward him or her for asking three times, then reducing it to two times, and then only one time. Finally, you can reward her or him for getting dressed without asking for any help at all. This is a useful strategy because it sets small goals rather than trying to eliminate a behavior all at once.

DIFFERENTIAL REINFORCEMENT OF INCOMPATIBLE OR ALTERNATIVE BEHAVIORS (DRI OR DRA)

DRI or DRA is reinforcing your child for doing an appropriate but incompatible behavior during your targeted activity. For example, if the problem behavior is pulling food off the shelves in the grocery store, you would reinforce your child for sitting in the cart, pushing the cart, putting food in the basket, holding the list, and so forth. All of these are appropriate behaviors and cannot be done at the same time as the inappropriate behavior. This strategy can teach a variety of behavior choices.

With a DRA, you pick specific behaviors to replace the problem behavior. For example, in the grocery store you could reinforce your child only when he or she is pushing the cart appropriately. This is a positive behavior to strengthen. In this way you can reduce the problem behavior and simultaneously replace it with a specific positive behavior.

HOW TO USE REINFORCEMENT

A reinforcer can be anything that your child likes and wants. Some reinforcers, called *primary reinforcers,* are more powerful because you do not have to learn to like them. Food is a primary reinforcer. Other reinforcers, called *secondary reinforcers,* can be powerful when we learn to like them. Attention or stickers are secondary reinforcers. There are two general rules. First, start by giving a lot of reinforcement and gradually decrease it over time. Second, work toward using secondary reinforcers, like stickers, by first pairing a primary reinforcer (like food) with the stickers and then gradually lessening the use of the food until you are only offering the stickers.

EXTINCTION

Extinction means to completely ignore a behavior so that it is no longer useful to your child. If a behavior doesn't work, your child will stop using it. You need to be prepared for your child to try even harder to make the undesirable behavior work before they will give it up, however. In other words, things get worse before they get better. If you choose to use extinction, be prepared for it to take time, make a plan for what you will do while you are ignoring the behavior, and get other people involved who are consistent in different settings. Do not be surprised if a behavior that disappeared suddenly reappears in the future. This is common. Be prepared to ignore it right away and it will disappear, usually quicker than before. Extinction only works if your child is using the behavior to get attention. If your child uses the behavior to escape a task or get an item, extinction will not be effective.

PUNISHMENT PROCEDURES

RESPONSE COST

This strategy removes reinforcement to reduce a problem behavior. For example, your child pulls all of the books off the shelves while watching a video. The response cost would be turning off the video when this behavior occurs. The video could come back on when the behavior stops or when the books have been placed back on the shelves.

TIME-OUT PROCEDURES

This involves time away from positive reinforcement, such as desired people, activities, or objects. This can happen with or without removing your child from the area. For example, your child could be seated in a chair away from the game table or taken to another room. There are differing opinions on how long time-outs should last (see Entry 5.7), but most will agree time-outs should be short and specific. For young children, a time-out could be as short as 1 minute. In my opinion, for older children, time-outs should not exceed 1 minute for every year of his or her age.

SUMMARY

There are many different strategies for changing behavior. The focus of changing inappropriate behavior always should be to replace it with an appropriate, useful behavior. Before designing a behavior plan, parents should refer to the resources listed here and work with a professional who has experience in developing behavior plans.

PRINT RESOURCES

Alberto, P. A., & Troutman, A. C. (2003). *Applied behavior analysis for teachers.* Upper Saddle River, NJ: Merrill/Prentice Hall.

Attwood, T. (2003). *Why does Chris do that? Some suggestions regarding the cause and management of the unusual behavior of children and adults with autism and Asperger syndrome.* Shawnee Mission, KS: Autism Asperger Publishing.

Hodgdon, L. A. (1999). *Solving behavior problems in autism.* Troy, MI: QuirkRoberts.

Maurice, C. (1996). *Behavioral intervention for young children with autism: A manual for parents and professionals.* Austin, TX: PRO-ED.

Myles, B. S. (2001). *Asperger syndrome and difficult moments: Practical solutions for tantrums, rage, and meltdowns.* Shawnee Mission, KS: Autism Asperger Publishing.

KEY TERMS

BEHAVIOR PLAN: A written plan that identifies intervention strategies to reduce inappropriate behaviors and increase appropriate behaviors

REINFORCER OR REWARD: Any item or activity that a child likes and wants

SEE ALSO THESE RELATED ENTRIES:

DEALING WITH SELF-STIMULATORY BEHAVIORS

Demitrio Fausto

EVERYONE engages in a behavior that could be described as *self-stimulatory*. Simple habits from nail biting or twirling your hair to playing video games or watching television can be called self-stimulatory behaviors. Many people enjoy the taste of a creamy milk-chocolate bar because it stimulates their taste buds and satisfies their chocolate craving. Even hobbies can be described as self-stimulatory behaviors. Many people enjoy working on cars and spend a majority of their free time under the hood of a car in the garage or front yard. Self-stimulatory behavior is a naturally occurring behavior for everyone, and anyone involved in developing programs for children with autism spectrum disorders (ASD) should keep this in mind as they search for ways to help these children decrease their self-stimulatory behaviors.

SELF-STIMULATORY BEHAVIOR AND ASD

Many children with ASD display behaviors that are described as repetitive or self-stimulatory. One characteristic of ASD is the tendency to do the same types of things, or behaviors, over and over. Some children with ASD like to spin things and watch them twirl around. Other children with ASD seem to enjoy the sensation of touching things or smelling certain objects over and over. Other self-stimulatory behaviors include body-rocking, clapping, hand flapping, looking at certain body parts or objects, and self-injury (e.g., banging the head, biting self). A self-stimulatory behavior is something the child does that seems to make him or her feel good.

COMPARISONS TO TYPICAL SELF-STIMULATORY BEHAVIOR

Some children with ASD seem to be unable to control their need to self-stimulate. A child's self-stimulatory behavior can interfere with learning new things, making friends, or even personal health and safety. For example, if a child with ASD enjoys the sensation of hitting objects with his or her hands and is unable to control this urge, it may cause difficulties when he or she is required to sit and attend appropriately in a classroom setting. It probably is best to look at what other children the same age are doing when trying to determine whether your child's self-stimulatory behavior is typical.

SOCIAL AND CULTURAL CONSIDERATIONS

Some self-stimulatory behaviors are viewed as appropriate, while others are viewed as inappropriate or at least inappropriate when done in certain situations. For example, at home a child may be allowed to jump up and down and make clicking noises with the tongue when in the living room. At school in the classroom, however, this type of behavior probably will not be appropriate. When looking at self-stimulatory behaviors, it is important to keep in mind the different cultures and customs of people. To some people there is nothing wrong with letting a child do what he or she wants to do as long as he or she is not jeopardizing his or her safety or that of others. To other people there is a time and a place for a child to do certain types of things.

THE ROLE OF REINFORCEMENT

When your child participates in a self-stimulatory behavior, he or she is looking for a way to satisfy, or reward, him- or herself with a certain need or want. For example, if your child enjoys the sensation of clapping his or her hands together, he or she will probably want to clap whenever feeling the need or desire to. Self-stimulatory behavior is perhaps one of the most difficult types of behavior to control because it essentially is controlled by your child and is the result of your child continually reinforcing or rewarding him- or herself. When developing a way to assist your child in decreasing a self-stimulatory behavior, keep in mind that it is better to replace the behavior with something else rather than try to stop the behavior all together. For example, if your child likes to flap his or her hands, give him or her something more appropriate (e.g., toy, book, magazine, computer) to do with the hands rather than simply demanding, "Quiet hands."

DETERMINING IF A BEHAVIOR IS SELF-STIMULATORY

Determining whether something a child does is self-stimulatory requires looking at all of the events that happen both before and after the behavior occurs. A behavior often may look as if it is serving to self-stimulate but also may serve as a way for your child to gain attention, communicate, or get out of doing something undesirable. Carefully looking at the events around the suspected self-stimulatory behavior will make it easier to determine whether the behavior actually is serving to self-stimulate your child.

EFFECTS OF EXERCISE ON SELF-STIMULATORY BEHAVIOR

INDIVIDUALS WITH ASD

Using exercise to decrease self-stimulatory behavior is an effective and practical tool in assisting some children with an ASD in managing some of their self-stimulatory needs. For example, jogging on the school playground or jumping on a small trampoline for 8 to 10 minutes prior to sitting at a desk in the classroom for 30 to 45 minutes can help a child in controlling his or her self-stimulatory behaviors. Providing a period of exercise for children with an ASD prior to going to a setting that requires them to manage their self-stimulatory behavior will probably decrease some, if not all, of their self-stimulatory behaviors immediately following the exercise. The exercise should be enough to get their heart rate up and maintain the rate anywhere from 8 to 20 minutes. Exercise can be whatever the child seems to enjoy, provided it is done at a pace faster than a normal walk. Before attempting to engage your child in any potentially high levels of exercise, discuss his or her present health with a doctor. It also is important to make the exercise activity fun and reinforcing. Try to incorporate plenty of interaction with other children or with adults.

LONG-TERM EFFECTS

The decrease in self-stimulatory behavior most likely will be noticed immediately following the exercise activity. Some people might think that the reason there is a decrease in a child's self-stimulatory behavior is because he or she is tired or fatigued. However, exercise does have a lasting effect throughout the day on reducing self-stimulatory behavior. Also, after exercising, a child with an ASD is more likely to focus on required tasks and activities in school, at home, and in the community. Exercise is good for the overall health of your child and can become a life-long interest that will increase his or her overall well-being.

SUMMARY

Self-stimulatory behavior is a normal part of our everyday lives. Some children with an ASD struggle with controlling their desire to self-stimulate, which can cause difficulties for them. When developing a plan to help decrease your child's self-stimulatory behavior, incorporating a period of exercise prior to the times when your child seems to have the most difficulties controlling the need to self-stimulate may be very useful. Exercise can be an effective tool not only in decreasing self-stimulatory behavior but also by increasing more appropriate behaviors in school, at home, and in the community.

WEB RESOURCES

Mercola.com (http://www.mercola.com/2001/oct/31/exercise_brain_power.htm)

Indiana Resource Center for Autism (http://www.iidc.indiana.edu/irca/SocialLeisure/exercisetp.html)

KEY TERMS

INTERVENTION: A clearly defined method of changing a behavior

REPETITIVE BEHAVIOR: A behavior that is repeated over and over again, such as body-rocking or hand-flapping

SELF-STIMULATORY BEHAVIOR: Any repetitive behavior that seems to serve the purpose of making the person feel good

SEE ALSO THESE RELATED ENTRIES:

GUIDELINES FOR EFFECTIVELY USING TIME-OUT

E. Amanda Boutot

DEALING with behaviors is one of the great challenges of raising a child. For parents of children with autism, this challenge may be more pronounced because of the nature of the disorder itself. Parents need to have a variety of strategies for effectively dealing with the inappropriate behaviors that their child sometimes exhibits. One such method that has been used by parents for quite some time is known as *time-out.* This entry discusses the definition of time-out, guidelines for effective use, and ideas on how to use it with your child.

DEFINITION

The science of behavior uses two methods for changing a behavior: reinforcement and punishment. By definition, reinforcement is a consequence that maintains or increases a behavior, while punishment is a consequence that decreases a behavior. Positive reinforcement is the same as rewards, and it is given in response to an appropriate behavior, whereas punishment is given for inappropriate behavior. Because time-out is given in response to inappropriate behavior in an effort to decrease the frequency, it is considered to be a punishment. Time-out is defined as "time out from reinforcement" meaning that during the time-out procedure, the child has no opportunity to earn a reward (Scheuermann & Webber, 2002). This entry focuses on this formal definition of time-out, but other forms that it sometimes takes also will be mentioned. For example, parents and teachers often wish for a child to "cool off" when he or she is angry or upset, and thus will send him or her to an area or his or her room as a time-out. This technically is not the same as the time-out discussed here because the purpose of sending the child to time-out is for the child to get him- or herself under control. Likewise, sending a child to time-out to "think about what he or she did wrong" is not time-out because the purpose also is for the child to think about the inappropriate behavior and presumably what to do instead the next time. Either of these approaches is an acceptable means of dealing with inappropriate behavior, but to work effectively as a punishment for a behavior, and thus decrease the likelihood that it will happen again, the following guidelines are recommended.

GUIDELINES FOR USING TIME-OUT

Using time-out effectively requires parents to adhere to certain guidelines, as follows. Time-out:
- must be immediate,
- must be understood by your child,
- must be short, and
- must return your child immediately to the situation or activity.

MUST BE IMMEDIATE

For time-out to be effective as a punishment strategy, it must occur immediately after the inappropriate behavior occurs. This especially is important for children with limited receptive language skills, so the child will learn that Behavior "X" leads to this consequence. If time-out is delayed, your child may not connect her or his inappropriate behavior with the consequence. When this happens, the punishment will not work to decrease that behavior, thus rendering it essentially useless.

MUST BE UNDERSTOOD BY THE CHILD

When you put your child in time-out, you must explain to him or her what is happening and why; for example, "Mary, you are going to time-out for hitting. No hitting." Using the same or similar words each time will ensure that your child begins to understand that Behavior "X" leads to this consequence. The better your child understands this, the more likely he or she will decrease the inappropriate behavior. Especially for children with limited receptive language, it is important to explain in simple and similar terms.

MUST BE SHORT

One of the reasons that time-out should be short is that if the child is returned to the situation or activity soon, he or she is less likely to try to use it as a means of escape. Teachers have long said that time-out should be the same number of minutes as the child's age. There are two reasons why this is an old-fashioned, outdated view of time-out. First, consider a girl who chronologically is age 16, but mentally is functioning as a 4-year-old. How long would she need to go to time-out? This quandary has no correct answer using the old formula. The second reason that the old formula is outdated and inappropriate is that it defeats the purpose of time-out. Placing a 6-year-old in time-out for 6 minutes will seem like an eternity to him or her. Not only may he or she not remember why he or she went to time-out in the first place, it is unlikely that the child will learn that Behavior "X" leads to time-out. In addition, many children left in time-out for a long time will either increase the intensity of their anger or tantrum or will enjoy the opportunity for some time to do whatever they want (for children with autism, this is the perfect opportunity to engage in self-stimulatory behaviors). This also defeats the purpose. There are differing opinions on how long time-out should last (see Entry 5.5). In my opinion, time-out should be no more than 2 minutes for the oldest child and no more than 10 to 15 seconds for very young or lower-functioning children. In this way, your child will be returned to the situation sooner and thus learn to associate Behavior "X" with this punishment.

MUST RETURN YOUR CHILD IMMEDIATELY TO THE SITUATION OR ACTIVITY

One of the dangers of using time-out is that your child will learn to use the behavior that leads to time-out as a means of escaping things he or she does not want to do. For example, if you routinely place your child in time-out for throwing things, he or she may begin to throw things to get out of taking a bath or getting dressed. Therefore, immediately after time-out is over, return your child to the original activity or situation. This way, he or she learns that the behavior will not get him or her out of anything. In addition, as soon as your child displays appropriate behavior after time-out, give a reward (even if only praise) so that he or she begins to associate appropriate behaviors with pleasant things and inappropriate behaviors with less pleasant things.

IDEAS FOR USING TIME-OUT WITH YOUR CHILD

There are no correct or incorrect methods for using time-out as long as the just-mentioned guidelines are met; however, some methods work better than others. These are discussed in this section, in order from least to most intrusive. The less-intrusive forms of time-out are suggested for less severe behaviors, whereas the more-intrusive forms should be reserved for serious infractions.

AS REMOVAL OF REINFORCEMENT RATHER THAN CHILD

When people think of time-out, they usually think of the child being removed from the situation to a room or to the corner. However, a very effective form of time-out is removing the situation, activity, or material from the child for a short period of time. For example, if the child is using his or her spoon to bang loudly on the table, taking away the spoon for a few seconds or a minute may be effective in teaching him or her that this is inappropriate. It is not necessary to always remove the child, especially for less serious behaviors for which it is easier to remove something else.

WHERE YOU ARE

Another example of a less-intrusive time-out is to place your child in time-out right where he or she is. For example, if your child is using her or his spoon to hit a younger brother, you can sit her or him down on the ground, cover his or her eyes or put his or her head down, and count to 10 (or 20). Immediately uncover the eyes or let your child go. Sometimes this must be repeated several times, but eventually your child will learn that hitting his or her brother is not as much fun as he or she thought.

IN A SEPARATE BUT VISIBLE PLACE

Time-out by covering your child's eyes for 1 or 2 minutes may not be possible. However, you do not have to send your child to his or her room. Having a special chair in your home that is just for time-out may work well. It allows you to watch your child and allows him or her to hear what he or she is missing, helping him or her see that going to time-out is not as much fun as behaving appropriately with the family.

IN A SEPARATE, OUT-OF-SIGHT PLACE

Finally, for serious infractions, parents may choose time-out in a separate room, such as the child's room or some other isolated place. This ensures that your child does not get inadvertently reinforced (rewarded) for the time-out by being able to see and hear everyone else. A caution about using this form of time-out: Do not keep your child in the place more than 2 minutes and make sure that the place is not reinforcing, making your child want to go to time-out.

SUMMARY

Time-out is an effective form of punishment for children who display inappropriate behaviors. Parents must be sure to stick to the guidelines so that the time-out will be effective. In addition, whenever possible, you should practice time-out with your child when he or she is not upset so that your child will know the expectations for behavior while in time-out, especially if you will be using a separate place. Finally, remember that time-out is time out from reinforcement. The alternate activity or situation must be more rewarding than the time-out. Using a lot of praise when your child is not in time-out for appropriate behavior is key to the success of time-out.

REFERENCE

Scheuermann, B., & Webber, J. (2002). *Autism: Teaching does make a difference.* Belmont, CA: Wadsworth.

KEY TERMS

Positive reinforcement: A reward is given in response to an appropriate behavior, given to maintain or increase the behavior

Punishment: Anything that decreases a behavior, although it only teaches a child what not to do

Time-out: Time out from reinforcement, meaning that during the time-out procedure, the child has no opportunity to earn a reward; given in response to inappropriate behaviors in an effort to decrease their frequency

SEE ALSO THESE RELATED ENTRIES:

USING NATURAL CONSEQUENCES TO TEACH YOUR CHILD

Matt Tincani

WHY IS IT IMPORTANT TO USE NATURAL CONSEQUENCES?

Natural consequences can be an important tool for teaching your child with autism. *Natural consequences* may be defined as the "pay-offs" that exist in your child's everyday environment that may be used to reward him or her for desired behaviors. To identify what your child's pay-offs may be, think of the things that he or she likes to do. These may include playing outside, listening to songs, watching videos, or eating a favorite food. Each of these activities has a skill or skills associated with it. For example, your child has to put on his or her shoes and ask permission to play outside. You can use this natural pay-off to teach him or her to tie the shoes and request to go outside. Natural consequences can be used to teach many skills to children with autism.

CONTRIVED VERSUS NATURAL CONSEQUENCES

In contrast to natural consequences, *contrived consequences* do not exist in your child's everyday environment unless somebody intentionally arranges them. Many educational programs for children with autism rely on contrived consequences. For example, a teacher might give edible rewards like candy to a child for tying his or her shoes. Edibles are contrived consequences because children do not normally receive candy when they tie their shoes. It sometimes is necessary to use contrived consequences because it is difficult to find things that motivate children with autism naturally. However, skills taught only with contrived consequences may not generalize to everyday settings. The child who learns to tie his or her shoes for candy is less likely to tie the shoes when it is time to play. Using natural consequences increases generalization of skills to natural settings and avoids the extra effort of finding and delivering contrived rewards.

HOW TO USE NATURAL CONSEQUENCES

IDENTIFY THINGS THAT YOUR CHILD LIKES IN HIS OR HER EVERYDAY ENVIRONMENT

To begin using natural consequences, you will need to identify some things that your child likes, such as everyday activities, toys, foods, or drinks. If you are not sure, spend some time observing your child to see what he or she does or have a family member help you make a list. Activities that many children prefer include meal and snack times, TV and videos, music, and favorite toys.

IDENTIFY SKILLS ASSOCIATED WITH PREFERRED ACTIVITIES

Every preferred activity has a skill and natural rewarding consequences associated with it. Table 1 identifies four preferred activities, natural consequences, and skills. These are everyday activities that many children enjoy. At the bottom of the table are two blank rows. Think of and write down two activities, natural consequences, and skills you could teach to your child.

The following questions may be helpful in identifying skills related to your child's preferred activities:

1. Does the activity involve asking someone for permission or help? How?
2. What does your child have to do before the activity can begin?
3. What does your child have to do to complete the activity?
4. What does your child have to do after the activity is over (e.g., clean up)?

SABOTAGING PREFERRED ACTIVITIES

It may be necessary to sabotage preferred activities to teach your child new skills. By *sabotage*, I mean purposefully arranging the activity so that your child must perform a new skill to complete it. For example, in a snack activity, you typically might place the straw in the drink box for your child. To sabotage the activity, you could deliberately not place the straw in the drink box so that your child has an opportunity to do it for him- or herself. In reading a book, you might usually turn the page without asking your child to identify what is in the picture. To sabotage this activity, delay turning the page for a second or two until your child has answered a simple question (e.g., "What color is the ball?"). The skill that you require should take only a short period of time (no

TABLE 1
SKILLS ASSOCIATED WITH PREFERRED ACTIVITIES

Activity	Natural	Skill
Eating snack	Eating cupcakes and drinking grape juice	• Setting the table • Asking for cupcakes • Asking for a drink • Putting a straw in the drink box
Reading books with mom or dad	• Hearing mom or dad read words out loud • Looking at pictures in the book	• Asking for a book • Asking for the page to be turned • Saying the names of colors, shapes, people, and animals
Watching videos	Seeing favorite movies	• Asking for a video • Asking for the TV and DVD player to be turned on
Trip to the store	• Car ride • Buying a favorite item	• Putting on shoes • Zipping up jacket • Asking to buy an item • Paying for the item

longer than 10 seconds) to perform. If it takes longer, your child may lose interest in the activity.

TEACHING TIPS

The following teaching tips will help your child learn new skills.

PROMPT IMMEDIATELY AT FIRST AND THEN DELAY YOUR PROMPTS

In the drink box example mentioned previously, the first time you require your child to place the straw in the drink box, he or she may not understand what is expected. Therefore, when you put the drink box on the table, immediately prompt him or her to remove the straw and place it in the box. Use the least intrusive prompt necessary. If your child responds to gestural prompts (e.g., pointing to the straw), use them. If your child does not respond to gestural prompts, you may need to use physical prompts (e.g., hand-over-hand guiding your child through the behavior). Physical prompts are more difficult to ease away from, so use them sparingly. As your child learns to do the skill on his or her own, wait a couple of seconds before you prompt. This will give your child an opportunity to beat the prompt and perform the skill independently.

BE AWARE OF PROMPT DEPENDENCE

Children with autism often become prompt dependent, seldom performing skills in the absence of prompts from parents or teachers. Prompt dependence is sometimes said to be a characteristic of children with autism; however, it is more likely to occur when verbal prompts are used too frequently. Because most children with autism have a difficult time understanding language, when you give even a simple instruction to your child (e.g., "Put on your jacket"), he or she may not understand what you are asking. If you find yourself frequently repeating instructions to your child, he or she may be prompt dependent. In most cases, it is preferable to start with a gestural prompt, which is a gesture that cues your child to perform a behavior. The most common example of a gestural prompt is pointing. If you want your child to put on his or her jacket before going outside, instead of saying it, you could point to the closet or jacket. If your child does not respond to the gestural prompt, you might use a light physical prompt that directs him or her to perform the behavior.

PRINT RESOURCES

Bondy, A., & Sultzer-Azaroff, B. (2000). *The Pyramid approach to education.* Newark, DE: Pyramid Educational Products.

Koegel, R. L., & Koegel, L. K. (1995). *Teaching children with autism: Strategies for initiating positive interactions and improving learning opportunities.* Baltimore: Brookes.

Sundberg, M. L., & Partington, J. W. (1998). *Teaching language to children with autism or other developmental disabilities.* Danville, CA: Behavior Analysts.

KEY TERMS

CONSEQUENCES: Responses to behaviors that either decrease or increase their future occurrence

PROMPTING: Cues given to assist a child in the successful completion of a task or skill

PROMPT DEPENDENCE: Phenomenon in which a child is unable or unwilling to perform a skill or task without adult prompts

SEE ALSO THESE RELATED ENTRIES:

DISCRETE TRIAL INSTRUCTION IN EARLY INTENSIVE BEHAVIORAL INTERVENTION

Stein K. Lund

EARLY intensive behavioral intervention (EIBI) for children with autism is a specialized field characterized by systematic application of behavioral principles (e.g., reinforcement and discrimination learning), instructional methods, and sophisticated curriculum development (Lund, 2001). An effective, yet controversial, instructional method within EIBI is *discrete trial instruction* (DTI), which emphasizes clear instruction and incremental teaching. As a component of a comprehensive intervention, DTI can be effective in promoting cognitive, language, and pragmatic skills. However, its role within the broader framework of EIBI may be unclear to many people. This entry discusses the role of discrete trial instruction in early intensive behavioral intervention.

APPLIED BEHAVIOR ANALYSIS AND EIBI

Applied behavior analysis (ABA) is concerned with improving socially important behaviors such as language, communication, social skills, and daily living skills. ABA is a broad field containing many methods and principles that have been effective as a foundation for early intervention for children with autism. Children with autism can make substantial and sustained gains in educational and intellectual functioning if behavioral intervention starts early (prior to the age of 5 years), is intensive (up to 40 hours per week), is comprehensive, and extends over consecutive years (Lovaas, 1987; McEachin, Smith, & Lovaas, 1993). EIBI is complex and involves comprehensive curricula (Leaf & McEachin, 1999) and a variety of instructional methods.

DISCRETE TRIAL INSTRUCTION

DTI is a particular application of basic learning principles designed to enhance skill acquisition and promote more efficient ways of learning (i.e., "learning how to learn"). The procedure may be understood as a general teaching framework that relies on two basic principles:

1. breaking down skills into smaller components, making them easier to learn; and
2. very clear instruction (i.e., unambiguous instruction). For instance, the concept of *prepositions* (e.g., under, on, next to, behind, in front of), which is very difficult for many children with autism to learn, may be broken into minimal components, starting with the name of the preposition (e.g., on) and gradually increasing in complexity as the child masters simpler steps ("on chair," "put the cup on the chair").

DTI is not restricted to simple skills such as imitation or specific response chains (i.e., dressing skills); it also may be used to teach a variety of sophisticated language skills, such as personal pronouns, descriptive sentences, answering the 5-W questions (who, what, where, when, why), conversational skills, and even basic perspective taking.

WHAT IS A DISCRETE TRIAL?

A discrete trial consists of a clear instruction (antecedent), the child's behavior, and an appropriate consequence. If the child responds correctly to the antecedent, the instructor provides reinforcement (i.e., any consequence that may increase the likelihood that the child will repeat the performance). If the child responds incorrectly, the instructor provides some other consequence that clearly marks the end of the trial, such as an instructional "no" or simply removing the instructional material. Each sequence is separated by a brief pause, often referred to as an *intertrial interval.*

DTI as an overall method, however, is not merely an unrelated bundle of individual trials. Rather, trials often are organized into complex systems that include error-correction strategies and the use of prompts (cues that are gradually removed as the child becomes more successful). Some versions of DTI, such as the "no-no-prompt error correction procedure," are elaborate and entail several phases, starting with continuous prompting (to reduce errors); strategies to reduce errors over time, enhance memory, and enhance proficiency (i.e., expanded trials); and a flexible shift of attention between tasks (Lund & Barnard, 2002). Use of such complex procedures requires considerable training and a thorough understanding of learning principles.

CONTROVERSIES SURROUNDING DTI

Despite its proven utility, DTI is controversial and frequently denounced. Common concerns include the claim that DTI causes rote and inflexible behavior, suppresses generalization, and engenders "splinter skills" with no practical value for the child.

Consequently, many clinicians prefer less-structured methods, such as natural environment teaching, that capitalize on teaching opportunities as they occur in more natural contexts (Sundberg & Partington, 1998).

However, unfavorable outcomes often attributed to DTI may be better understood as a result of the intervention as a whole rather than the method itself. Issues such as poor program design and inconsistent use may contribute to poor outcomes observed in some programs where DTI is employed. If DTI is used in isolation from broader treatment concerns, it could contribute to rote and inflexible behavior. In other words, there is nothing in DTI that causes the previously mentioned problems. Keep in mind that DTI is an implementation method, not an intervention program, and its effectiveness depends on the overall quality of the program of which it is a part. Unfortunately, DTI and EIBI are sometimes used interchangeably, and this error contributes to false claims about DTI.

DTI IN EARLY INTENSIVE BEHAVIORAL INTERVENTION

Terms such as *discrete trial treatment* or *discrete trial intervention* are common but misguided ways of referring to EIBI. Such terms single out a method to stand for a broader intervention. To appreciate the role of DTI in EIBI, it may be useful to think of the field in terms of three interrelated components: curriculum, analysis, and implementation (Lund, 2001).

Curriculum is the content of the intervention (i.e., what to teach). A curriculum in EIBI should be very comprehensive and address all general areas of development (language, communication, cognitive skills, social skills, play skills, and preacademics). It should specify steps and the connections between skill sequences. In addition to specific content, a curriculum should address "tool skills" (e.g., attention, memory, persistence) and qualities such as fluency (accuracy plus speed), variability, and generative learning (the ability to perform untaught skills in new situations).

Analysis includes the general concepts and principles of applied behavior analysis and is a cornerstone of the intervention. Analysis involves assessing the child's interaction with his or her environment (e.g., functional analysis), skills, deficits, and learning characteristics. Moreover, the term *analysis,* which means "decomposition into parts," is concerned with breaking complex skills down into teachable units.

Implementation is the practical application of instructional methods (e.g., DTI) and the overall intervention structure. Practical application concerns issues such as selecting, using, and adjusting teaching methods (i.e., matching a method to the target skill) and arrangement of an instructional session (e.g., breaks, interspersing mastered and target skills, and data collection). Intervention structure is the organization and coherence of the overall program, including quality control, considerations of when to teach a skill, and use of a curriculum protocol to accommodate individual learners.

DTI is neither a curriculum nor an analytic tool. It is an instructional method and should therefore be classified as a component of implementation. This classification helps us to understand the role of DTI in EIBI and to appreciate the complexity of the field.

SUMMARY

EIBI for children with autism is a complex approach based on the concepts and principles of applied behavior analysis. DTI is one of many instructional methods that can be used in EIBI. Its effectiveness depends on other factors, such as quality of curriculum development (competency of the curriculum designer), application of complementary instructional methods, and ongoing analysis and adjustments. As with any method, DTI has limitations, but a careful analysis reveals that much of the criticism of DTI may be due to inadequate curriculum development and inappropriate use, rather than to the method itself.

REFERENCES

Leaf, R., & McEachin, J. J. (1999). *A work in progress: Behavior management strategies and a curriculum for intensive treatment of autism.* Austin, TX: PRO-ED.

Lovaas, O. I. (1987). Behavioral treatment and normal educational and intellectual functioning in young children with autism. *Journal of Consulting and Clinical Psychology, 55,* 3–9.

Lund, S. K. (2001). Content and contingencies: Considerations regarding curriculum development for young children with autism. *Behavior Analysts Today, 3,* 187–191.

Lund, S. K., & Barnard, J. C. (2002, May). *The "no-no prompt" procedure as a complex system of implementation.* Paper presented at the 28th annual convention for the Association for Behavior Analysis, Toronto, Canada.

McEachin, J. J., Smith, T., & Lovaas, O. J. (1993). Long-term outcome for children who received early intensive behavioral treatment. *American Journal on Mental Retardation, 97,* 359–372.

Sundberg, M. L., & Partington, J. W. (1998). *Teaching language to children with autism and other developmental disabilities.* Danville, CA: Behavior Analysts.

KEY TERMS

Discrete trial instruction: A particular application of basic learning principles designed to facilitate learning; emphasizes clarity of instruction and the teaching of skills in an incremental manner and is one of the many instructional methods used in EIBI

Early intensive behavioral intervention: A specialized clinical field characterized by systematic applications of behavior analysis principles, instructional methods, and comprehensive and sophisticated curriculum development

SEE ALSO THIS RELATED ENTRY:

ASSESSING AND TEACHING IMITATION SKILLS

Michelle A. Anderson, Susan M. Silvestri, Natalie J. Allen, Corinne M. Murphy, Charles L. Wood, and William L. Heward

WHEN a child (or an adult) does what someone else is doing, he or she may be imitating that person. Technically, imitation is behavior that corresponds one-to-one to a model or example (i.e., the child does what another person is doing or has just done). Numerous examples of imitation are easily seen in the everyday life of a child including the toddler who says, "Hello, Uncle Rick!" to a man at the front door after his big brother just said the same words or the preschooler who follows along with his toy lawnmower while his dad mows the lawn.

Typically developing children naturally learn to imitate the behavior of others, and they use imitation to learn countless language, play, self-help, and social-emotional skills. Children also can learn undesirable behaviors by imitating inappropriate behavior. In the case of some children with developmental disabilities, undesirable imitation can occur. This can be seen when a child frequently repeats exactly what she has heard others say but rarely says those words in a functional way (called *echolalia*). However, the benefits of teaching a child with autism to imitate far outweigh the potential for the imitation of undesirable behaviors or the development of noncommunicative imitation.

THE IMPORTANCE OF IMITATION

Imitation enables children (and adults) to learn from observing others. When unsure how to behave in a new situation, such as visiting a foreign culture or attending a new church, we immediately look to see what other people are doing and adjust our actions to match theirs. Imitating the behavior of others enables us to fit in quickly and learn the skills needed to function in the new setting. Children frequently find themselves in new situations, especially as they enter school and are introduced to new routines, cultures, and peer groups.

Imitation also is important because it allows children to benefit from model prompts when learning new skills. When teaching a new skill (e.g., following instructions such as "Clap your hands"), a parent can model the correct response as a prompt (parent says, "Clap your hands," and claps her or his own hands). Model prompts are only effective for children who can imitate.

ASSESSING YOUR CHILD'S IMITATION SKILLS

You can determine whether your child needs imitation instruction by conducting the following assessment. Before starting, carefully read all of the steps and gather the necessary materials. Conduct the assessment while sitting at a table facing your child at a quiet time that is free from distractions.

1. Gain your child's attention by calling his or her name or showing a favorite toy.
2. Say, "Do this," and clap your hands.

3. If your child claps his or her hands, immediately provide praise and a tickle, hug, or small treat and go to Step 4. If your child does not imitate your action, repeat Step 2. If your child does not imitate your action on the second try, proceed to Step 4.
4. Repeat Steps 2 and 3 until you have tested 10 different actions (e.g., touch head, stand up, stack blocks, hit drum, jump, feed baby doll).
5. Keep a record of your child's response to each action. Note whether your child (a) correctly imitates the behavior, (b) approximates an imitation, or (c) does not imitate. If your child imitates your action on the first or second try, count the trial as correct.
6. If your child imitated 7 or more of your actions, read the section on Applications to learn some ways to take advantage of your child's good imitation skills. If your child imitated less than 7 of the 10 actions you modeled, read the next section for suggestions on how to teach your child to imitate.

TEACHING YOUR CHILD TO IMITATE

Set aside at least one 10- to 15-minute session each day for imitation training with your child. Instruction should occur in an area free from distractions where you and your child can sit facing each other, with materials for modeling actions (e.g., the toys used during the assessment) and things your child likes (e.g., preferred toys or edible treats) to use as reinforcers close at hand. Early imitation instruction should be done in a structured manner. Discrete trial training is one effective way to help children with autism learn new skills. Entry 5.9 discusses this method. Learning a new skill may go slowly, especially in the beginning.

TABLE 2
NONVERBAL AND VERBAL IMITATION SKILLS

Nonverbal Imitation Skill		Verbal Imitation Skill	
(Prerequisite skills: sits at table and attends to adult)		(Prerequisite skills: usually imitates a nonverbal model and can produce several different vocal sounds)	
SKILL	EXAMPLE	SKILL	EXAMPLE
gross motor	slaps hands, touches head	sound combinations	/da/, /up/, /sa/, /ip/
fine motor with objects	strings beads, puts shirt on doll	single-syllable words	cup, ball, top, hi
fine motor	crosses fingers, points	multisyllable words	apple, story, computer, elephant
oral motor	sticks out tongue, puckers lips	multiword phrases	"I like juice." "My name is Sam."
chains	does two or more modeled actions in sequence (stacks blocks and claps)	volume and pitch	loud and quiet volume, high and low pitch

During this time, give your child a lot of praise and reinforcement for taking small steps toward the goal of consistent and accurate imitation.

WHAT TO TEACH

Table 2 gives examples of nonverbal and verbal skills that should be included in an imitation training. Because physical prompts and hand-over-hand guidance can be used with motor skills, it usually is easier to teach a nonimitative child to imitate nonverbal actions than it is to teach verbal imitation. Within the area of nonverbal actions, most children will learn to imitate gross motor (large muscle) movements (e.g., walking) easier than they will learn to imitate fine motor (small muscle) movements (e.g., writing) and oral motor skills (e.g., speech). Therefore, the sequence of gross motor, fine motor, oral motor, and then verbal skills is often the most effective for teaching imitation. However, information about your child's performance during the training sessions should dictate the sequence and speed of instruction.

APPLICATIONS

The following are some ways to take advantage of your child's ability to imitate to teach him or her new skills.

Requesting Things. Telling others what we want or need is a very important skill. The child who can imitate words (or approximations) can be taught to request items through modeling the response. For example, if your child looks at an out-of-reach juice cup, you can say to him or her, "Say *juice* (or *cup*)." When he or she says *"juice,"* reinforce this response by giving your child the juice cup. Slowly withdraw your model over time by reducing the amount of the word that you provide as a prompt (e.g., "Say *ju__*" and then "Say *j__*").

Naming Objects. Imitation can be used to teach your child to label important things in his or her world. For example, point to a ball and say, "Say *ball*." When your child repeats, "ball," immediately reinforce the response (e.g., "That's right, it is a ball! You're so smart!"). The more often your child says the names of objects in the presence of those objects and receives reinforcement for doing so, the more likely he or she is to begin naming objects without an imitative model.

Play Skills. Imitation can be used to teach appropriate play skills. During free play, prompt your child to imitate your actions or the actions of another child. For example, if another child is dumping blocks from a dump truck, tell your child, "Do what Jimmy is doing." At first you may need to also do the action and use the instruction, "Do this."

Observational Learning. It is important to generalize your child's imitation skills to other children. Once your child learns to cue into and do what other children are doing, he or she will be more able to follow along in school and similar settings. For example, if the teacher gives lengthy directions about a project that your child does not understand, he or she can still be successful by checking to see what the other children are doing and following along.

It may be necessary to build some instruction with a peer model into your discrete trial training sessions; however, you may be able to accomplish generalization to other children in the natural setting by using a child who helps out because he or she "knows the game." This child will use the right words ("Do this") and perform simple actions. Teach this child how to reinforce your child for responding. With time and repeated practice opportunities, structured guidance will be needed less and less for your child to cue into his or her peers.

PRINT RESOURCES

Leaf, R., & McEachin, J. (1999). *A work in progress: Behavior management strategies and a curriculum for intensive behavioral treatment of autism.* Austin, TX: PRO-ED.

Maurice, C., Green, G., & Luce, S. C. (1996). *Behavioral interventions for young children with autism: A manual for parents and professionals.* Austin, TX: PRO-ED.

Striefel, S. (1998). How to teach through modeling and imitation (2nd ed.). Austin, TX: PRO-ED.

KEY TERMS

IMITATION: A behavior with one-to-one correspondence to a model or example (i.e., the child does what another person is doing or has just done); enables children (and adults) to learn from observing others

MODEL PROMPT: Modeling the correct response as a prompt when teaching a new skill

NONVERBAL IMITATION: Imitating gross motor, fine motor, and oral motor movements

POSITIVE REINFORCEMENT: A reward given in response to an appropriate behavior; given to maintain or increase the behavior

VERBAL IMITATION: Imitating several different vocal sounds, from single sounds to multiple-word sounds

SEE ALSO THESE RELATED ENTRIES:

USING PRAISE AND APPROVAL EFFECTIVELY

Charles L. Wood, Natalie J. Allen,
Susan M. Silvestri, Michelle A. Anderson,
Corinne M. Murphy, and William L. Heward

PRAISE and approval are positive ways to improve your child's behavior. This entry provides a rationale for using praise and approval and offers suggestions for using them effectively.

WHAT ARE PRAISE AND APPROVAL?

Praise and approval are things you do and say to show you value someone's behavior that you would like to see repeated in the future. Examples include the following:

Things You Do	Things You Say
Pats on the back	"Sharing the book with your sister was excellent."
"High fives"	"I love it when you put away your toys, Brady!"
Hug	"You've been a super helper! Thanks!"
Tickle	"Katy, that was great asking for help!"

Things You Do	Things You Say
Give a thumbs-up	"Wow! That's sure a neat drawing, Cooper!"
Smile and wink	"Henry, you're playing so nicely with your brother!"

WHY PRAISE AND APPROVAL ARE IMPORTANT

Providing praise and approval for children's behavior has at least five important benefits:

- *Increases appropriate behavior.* When your child has done something you would like to see her or him do more often (e.g., saying "Please" and "Thank you," putting toys back on the shelf), attending to that behavior with praise and approval makes it more likely he or she will repeat it in the future.

- *Clarifies your expectations.* For example, when your child has hung up his or her coat, you quickly show a "thumbs-up" sign and say, "Thanks for hanging up your coat!" This lets your child know that hanging up his or her coat is something you expect and appreciate.

- *Decreases acting out or misbehaving to get your attention.* Children who lack attention for behaving appropriately often misbehave (e.g., scream, throw toys) to get their parents' attention. Using praise and approval to reward desirable behaviors makes it less likely that your child will have to misbehave to get your attention.

- *Makes your child want to be with you.* When you become a source of praise and approval, your child will seek your attention and engage in behaviors that please you.

- *Feels good for you and your child.* Positive parenting makes you feel good, and the attention your child receives will make him or her also feel good.

HOW DO PRAISE AND APPROVAL WORK?

Positive reinforcement is the underlying principle that makes praise and approval effective. Positive reinforcement occurs when a behavior is followed by an event that increases the likelihood of the behavior occurring in the future. If your praise and approval increases your child's good behavior, positive reinforcement has occurred. For more information on positive reinforcement, see Entry 5.4.

CHARACTERISTICS OF EFFECTIVE PRAISE AND APPROVAL

Praise and approval are more effective when they have the following characteristics.

- *Immediate.* Praise and approval are more effective when given immediately after a child engages in a desirable behavior. (If you do not have the opportunity or forget to show your approval when the desired behavior has just occurred, it is still better to praise your child for her or his good behavior at a later time than to ignore the behavior altogether.)
- *Specific.* Praise and approval should identify specific behaviors. For example, saying, "Thank you for putting your books away, Jacob," is more effective than saying, "Good job." (However, saying, "Good job," is better than saying nothing at all.)
- *Frequent.* Frequent praise and approval are important for helping a child learn and maintain new behaviors. Use praise

and approval to catch him or her being good as often as you can.

- *Varied.* Avoid always using the same comments and gestures to show praise and approval. Varying what you do and what you say can make praise and approval more effective.

- *Enthusiastic and natural.* Praise and approval should be delivered with enthusiasm and energy. For example, when your child is playing in the sandbox, you might exclaim, "Whoa, that's a really neat castle you're making, Brittany!" Do not worry if your praise and approval sounds unnatural or wooden at first. The more often you do it, the better you will get.

SUGGESTIONS FOR USING PRAISE AND APPROVAL

The following suggestions can help you use praise and approval effectively:

- *Remind yourself.* It can be difficult to remember to use praise and approval. Write short messages, such as, "Catch Tyler being good!" or "Praise a lot!" on sticky notes and put them in places you frequently look (e.g., the refrigerator, a mirror, on the TV remote). Put a few "smiley" face or star stickers in your car and around the house (e.g., child's bedroom door, swing set, clock). Each time you see a note or sticker, you will be reminded to use praise and approval.

- *Praise yourself.* It may sound funny, but praising yourself for using praise and approval can help you do it more often. Keep a simple tally of the number of times you give praise and approval for your child's behavior. An easy way to do this is to place 10 pennies in a pocket and transfer 1 penny to another pocket each time you give praise or approval. At the end of the day, record your total in a notebook and monitor your progress over time. Parents can reward themselves and each other for using praise and can compete to see who uses it the most. For example, the parent who delivers the most praise or approval that day does not have to do the dishes.

- *Combine praise and approval with other rewards.* Initially, your praise and approval might not serve as positive reinforcement. Praise and approval need to be combined with other rewards before they become effective reinforcers for some children. In the beginning you may need to give your child one of his or her favorite snacks or toys at the same time you praise his or her behavior. Repeated pairing of your praise and approval with other rewards will strengthen their effectiveness as reinforcers.

- *Encourage others to use praise and approval with your child.* There are many occasions when you are not with your child, so encourage teachers, siblings, grandparents, neighbors, and friends to catch your child being good. Not only can this ensure that your child receives a lot of praise and approval, but it can help his or her new behaviors to generalize to new situations. For information on promoting the generalization of newly learned skills to other settings and situations, see Entry 7.4.

- *Think small and celebrate small successes.* Do not expect big changes in your child's behavior right away. If your child does not like to share toys with other children, do not expect her or him to begin playing cooperatively with others just because you have praised her or him once or twice for sharing a toy. However, providing praise and approval for any attempt and approximation of cooperative play and sharing (e.g., "You can use my crayon") will make it more likely that your child learns to do so. You will make more progress if you select small, reachable goals. If your child does not like vegetables, praise him or her for eating one or two green beans before you expect him or her to eat them all. Each time your child takes a small step toward a more significant learning goal or accomplishment, celebrate his or her success and yours.

PRINT RESOURCES

Hall, R. V., & Hall, M. L. (1998). *How to use systematic attention and approval* (2nd ed.). Austin, TX: PRO-ED.

Latham, G. I. (1994). *The power of positive parenting*. North Logan, UT: P&T Inc.

Patterson, G. R. (1977). *Living with children: New methods for parents and teachers*. Champaign, IL: Research Press.

WEB RESOURCES

The DARE Program: 100 Ways to Praise a Child (http://www.sayno.com/child.html)

KEY TERMS

POSITIVE REINFORCEMENT: A reward given in response to an appropriate behavior; given to maintain or increase a behavior

PRAISE AND APPROVAL: Positive ways to improve your child's behavior; these are things you do and say to show you value someone's behavior and that you would like to see it repeated in the future

SEE ALSO THESE RELATED ENTRIES:

IMPROVING COMPLIANCE WITH CHOICE

Stephanie M. Peterson and Renee K. Van Norman

HAVE you ever had the experience of asking your child to pick up his or her toys or head up to bed to receive a loud, "No!" and a stomp of the foot? Displays of disruptive behavior are common in the face of difficult activities or undesirable chores, especially for children with autism. For some children, these behaviors interfere with their ability to participate in day-to-day activities. Sometimes, it helps to provide choices between or within activities. This entry describes ways you can provide choices to help your child comply.

PROVIDING CHOICES AMONG ACTIVITIES

One way to give your child choices is to allow her or him to pick among different activities. We suggest using this type of choice making in situations where it is not imperative that your child complete a particular activity. For example, if you have a list of chores, you could give your child a choice of which chores to complete.

PROVIDING CHOICES WITHIN ACTIVITIES

When it is important that your child complete a chore or activity, providing choice among activities may not be a useful strategy. For example, if your child must go to school, allowing him or her to choose between staying in pajamas or getting dressed will probably not work to your advantage! In this case, getting dressed is not a choice. However, you can still provide choices within the routine of getting dressed. For example, allow your child to choose which outfit to wear.

Some academic situations can prove to be troublesome for children with autism. Providing choices in these situations may decrease problem behaviors. For example, you could provide your child with a choice of writing utensils (e.g., pen, pencil, crayon, marker).

PROVIDING CHOICES
IN THE SEQUENCE OF ACTIVITIES

Sometimes it is helpful to allow children to determine the sequence in which they will complete activities. This can be a useful strategy when you want your child to complete several different activities and not to opt completely out of a specific activity. For example, if you want your child to make her or his bed and pick up dirty clothes, you might tell her or him that both tasks need to be completed but that he or she can choose which one to complete first. If your child follows a work or activity schedule, allowing your child to choose the sequence is an excellent opportunity to provide choice. For example, some children with autism may follow a picture or written schedule that indicates what activity is coming up next. Some parents find it very useful to allow their children to select which activities will occur when, and to place the pictures representing those activities on the picture schedule in the selected sequence. Providing choice in this situation is important.

PROVIDING CHOICES AMONG REWARDS

Quite often, parents will use reward systems to help motivate their children to complete daily activities and routines. Similarly, parents may offer a highly motivating activity that will follow the completion of a dreaded chore. You can increase the likelihood that a reward will be highly motivating by allowing your child to select the reward. For example, when sitting down to complete a difficult or unfavorable activity with your child, you might ask what he or she would like to do when finished with the activity.

PROBLEMS OF AND LIMITATIONS IN PROVIDING CHOICES

MY CHILD DOES NOT KNOW HOW TO MAKE CHOICES. CAN I STILL USE CHOICE-MAKING?

If your child does not know how to make choices, you will need to teach this skill. First, identify some favorite items (e.g., candy, popcorn, preferred toys) and teach your child some way to indicate that he or she wants the item. For example, if your child can talk, you might teach him or her to say, "Want candy." If your child does not talk, you could teach her or him to reach for or point to the item. You may choose to teach your child a simple sign to ask for an item, such as "more" or "please." When your child can reliably indicate that he or she wants an item, you can begin working on choice-making.

When first teaching choice-making, we have found it helpful to begin by offering choices that are extremely different from each other. For example, you might begin by pairing the highly preferred item you used to teach the "want" request with a less preferred item, such as some kind of bitter or sour candy. Hold both items up and say, "Which one do you want?" If your child reaches for the favorite candy, give it to him or her. If he or she reaches for the undesirable item, give that item. Repeat this over and over, making sure to change which hands the preferred and nonpreferred items are in (so that your child does not learn to always choose what is on the right or the left side).

MY CHILD ALWAYS CHOOSES THE SAME THING, AND IT IS NOT THE CHOICE I WANT HIM OR HER TO MAKE. WHAT CAN I DO TO GET MY CHILD TO MAKE BETTER CHOICES?

Let's assume you offer your child a choice between picking up toys and working on making the bed. Your child always chooses making the bed. You might be happy that he or she makes the bed, but you would rather he or she picks up the toys. One way is to make the toy chore easier by requiring your child to pick up only one toy. When your child begins to consistently choose to pick up toys, you could then increase the number of toys that need to be picked up.

It also is possible to influence your child's choices by changing the rewards associated with each choice. For example, if you have a reward system in place for completing activities, you can provide more of the reward when your child chooses to complete the task you want him or her to do. Similarly, you can vary the quality of the reward, giving an extra special reward for completing the less-preferred task.

WHEN IS THE BEST TIME TO TEACH CHOICE-MAKING?

Some people make the mistake of offering choices only following problem behavior. For example, while at the supermarket, your child begins to throw a tantrum because he or she cannot have a desired cereal. You might then offer a choice of two other cereals that the child can have. This is not the best time to offer a choice. If a choice-making opportunity follows a tantrum, the child actually might get rewarded for throwing the tantrum because it resulted in a positive outcome (i.e., a choice-making opportunity). A better strategy would be to use choice-making proactively—before a problem behavior occurs. In the previous example, it would be better if you offered a choice of cereals immediately upon entering the cereal aisle rather than waiting until a problem behavior occurred. This means, however, that you have to be on your toes and ready to predict when a problem behavior might happen so that you can use choice-making effectively.

SUMMARY

Why does choice-making work to improve children's behavior and compliance? To date the research has not been very clear on this subject. Some people think that choice-making allows children to have some control over their environment. Others think that choice-making allows children to obtain more preferred activities and rewards. Another view is that providing choices may change the child's view of the demand you are making. For example, when a nonpreferred chore or activity is presented as a choice or an option, perhaps the chore or task becomes more preferred. No one really knows for sure at this point. The message is that choice-making can be a very effective way to get your child to agree to your requests. Even if you do feel like you are giving up some control and handing it over to your child, keep in mind that you still are in control of the choices you offer. You still are maintaining some control over the chores and activities your child completes. Providing choices simply allows your child to share in that control a little bit.

KEY TERMS

CHOICE-MAKING: A child's ability to select items or activities that he or she prefers

COMPLIANCE: Responding to requests or commands correctly within a reasonable amount of time

SEE ALSO THESE RELATED ENTRIES:

SECTION
6

ISSUES IN SOCIAL SKILLS

SOCIAL STORIES

Shannon Crozier

CHILDREN with an autism spectrum disorder (ASD) often have difficulty learning social skills and understanding social situations. Pictures, words, and other visual cues often are much easier for them to understand. A *social story* is a tool for using their visual learning strengths to teach social skills and understanding. Social stories are easy to use, are easy to make, and can be effective for changing behavior.

WHAT IS A SOCIAL STORY?

A social story is a short story written specifically for your child to provide detailed and accurate information about a social situation. It is written from the child's perspective, and the text is easily within his or her comprehension level. Ideally, a story should be written so that a child can read it independently. However, an adult can read the story aloud to a child who does not read. Social stories can be written for any social situation. The following is an example of a social story for waiting your turn.

> My family plays games together after dinner.
> We sit at the table to play.
> Everyone gets a turn to play the game.
> When it is my turn, I can role the dice and move my marker.
> After I move, I have to wait for everyone else to have a turn.

When I wait, I will keep my hands in my lap.
I can watch my family take their turns.
I can think of my favorite song.
I will do my best to wait until it is my turn again.
My family will be happy when I wait my turn.

An effective social story follows some simple guidelines. Before writing a story, you must understand the problem situation from your child's perspective. If the story gives the wrong information, it will not be effective. For example, if your child grabs game pieces because he or she likes how they feel, a story about waiting your turn will not help. A story about other things to touch would be more effective.

TYPES OF SOCIAL STORY SENTENCES

A social story has three types of sentences: *descriptive, directive,* and *perspective.* A descriptive sentence describes the setting or the context of the social interaction. In the story example just given, "My family plays games together after dinner" and "We sit at the table to play" are descriptive sentences.

A directive sentence gives specific details of desired behavior. These should be stated positively, telling the child exactly what to do. For example, "When I wait, I will keep my hands in my lap" gives a positive direction. "I will not touch the board" does not tell the child what to do instead.

A perspective sentence describes the thoughts or actions of other people in the story. "My family will be happy when I wait my turn" gives the child information about his or her family's feelings. Perspective sentences are important because they help children understand confusing social cues. However, you should only include one or two of these sentences in a story.

Each page of the storybook should have only one idea, which might mean that each page has only one sentence. The text should be simple and large enough for your child to read and understand it independently. You can write social stories using only text or you can pair text with simple pictures or icons. Using pictures depends on the needs and learning style of your child. If you do use pictures or icons, follow these guidelines:

- Make sure your child understands pictures.
- Use simple line drawings in black and white.
- Use only one to two pictures or items on each page.

USING A SOCIAL STORY

How you use a social story is just as important as how you write it. It also will depend on your child and how he or she learns. The first time you introduce the story, sit beside your child and read the story with him or her or listen as he or she reads. Ask questions to make sure your child understands what is being read, for example, "Where should you keep your hands when you wait your turn?" After the first reading, you do not need to ask questions again.

At first your child should read the story every day. The time when it is read can vary: It can be read at the same time each day or right before the activity described in the story. Some children will read it only a few times before learning the target behavior. Some children will need to read the story before every activity. Other children will read it for a few weeks and then need to review it occasionally. It is a good idea to keep the social story somewhere that your child can see and read it whenever he or she wants.

BENEFITS OF SOCIAL STORIES

Social stories are easy and quick to make. They can be written on any topic, and it is easy to make multiple copies for home, for school, and for community outings. Because they also are easy to understand, everyone can have the same expectations of your child. You can use more than one social story at a time. Introduce them one at a time and allow your child several days or a couple of weeks to adjust to each new story. Finally, children usually enjoy reading stories about themselves. This makes learning new behaviors a positive experience.

Social stories also can be used with children who do not yet read. A story can be created using only photographs or line drawings showing the sequence of events, or photos or line drawings can be paired with text. This way, your child can rely on the pictures while becoming familiar with simple text.

SUMMARY

Social stories offer a high level of flexibility in meeting the individual needs of children with an ASD. In addition to being easy to make and use, they can complement other behavioral interventions. This makes them an ideal strategy to include in a multi-component behavior plan.

PRINT RESOURCES

Gray, C. (1994). *Comic book conversations*. Arlington, TX: Future Horizons.

Gray, C. (2000). *The new social story book: Illustrated edition*. Arlington, TX: Future Horizons.

KEY TERMS

COMPREHENSION LEVEL: The level of text difficulty that a child can read and understand independently

MULTICOMPONENT BEHAVIOR PLAN: A written plan that identifies intervention strategies for changing multiple behaviors across different settings

SOCIAL CUES: The nonverbal and unspoken rules of social interaction, including the use of eye contact, tone of voice, personal space, body language, and turn taking

SEE ALSO THESE RELATED ENTRIES:

TEACHING SOCIAL SKILLS THROUGH PLAY

Jessica E. Frieder, Tabitha J. Kirby,
and Jennifer Migliorini

Social skills are critical for all developing children. Problems with social skills will result in conflicts with other children and adults. This entry describes ways to teach social skills through play, specifically, turn taking and cooperative games.

TEACHING SOCIAL SKILLS DURING TURN-TAKING ACTIVITIES

The first step is to determine the social skills your child needs to develop. Critical social skills for most children include turn taking, initiating and maintaining interactions, accepting "no" responses, and sharing and cooperating. After you have made a decision about what types of social skills are important for your child, you need to combine them with play activities. Activities that involve turn taking provide learning opportunities for a variety of social skills. Some examples of turn-taking games/ activities include the Go Fish card game, a memory game, Connect Four, Candy Land, Chutes n' Ladders, and checkers, or a variety of pretend play activities. Turn taking gives children the chance to learn all types of social skills by interacting with one another through the activity. Children may become better at talking with other children and adults and learn cultural rules about social proximity and intrusion, appropriate winning and losing behaviors, joining in, and solving problems effectively. The following is an example of a situation where the desired skill is joining in.

> Keya and Cindy are playing Go Fish. Sam comes along and decides that he wants to play too, but they are in the middle of a game. What can Sam do? This is a great opportunity for Sam to learn or practice the proper skills of joining in.

- Decide if the game is already in progress (in this case, we know that the other two children are already playing a game).
- Politely interrupt by saying something like, "Excuse me," and ask in a pleasant tone of voice if he could join in the next game.
- After receiving a response, say "Thanks" or "OK."
- Wait quietly to join in until the next round.

If Sam did a good job of demonstrating these skills, you would be sure to praise him. If not, do not forget about the steps for redirecting and correcting—praise, state the skill, and state why it is important.

TEACHING SOCIAL SKILLS DURING COOPERATIVE ACTIVITIES

Another way to combine social skills through play is with cooperative play games or activities. Cooperative play is when two or more children are working together toward one goal. Cooperative play enhances the idea of teamwork or children working together to obtain a common goal or achievement. Each team member should be encouraged to be an involved part of the team to produce the end result. Examples of cooperative team games include group games like freeze tag, kickball, or tug of war and classroom games such as "Heads Up, Seven Up," or round-robin spelling games. Cooperative play activities involve many of the same opportunities to learn and practice different social skills offered by turn-taking play, but cooperative play also may provide unique chances for teaching other social skills. For example, children may be given the chance to learn and practice the social skills of dealing with teasing or being left out, accepting "no" for an answer, and interacting positively in a collective manner on a team. The following is an example regarding teasing:

> The sibling of a child with autism has several friends over to the house. They decide to play a board game, and they must divide into two teams. The child with autism wants to play with the kids, but Billy, a neighbor, doesn't want her to participate. Billy turns to the rest of the kids and says, "We all know that stupid Sally can't play because she doesn't know how to follow the rules!" What can Sally do?

- Decide if she is being teased.
- Think about ways to deal with the teasing (e.g., accept it, make a joke of it, tell the other person it hurt her feelings).
- Choose the best way (a way that will not encourage more teasing, aggression, or withdrawal) and do it.

The game is supposed to be cooperative, and winning is based on teamwork. In this case, Sally might be able to learn and practice how to handle teasing. And of course, do not forget that as the adult you should praise Sally for learning how to get along with others.

RESOURCES

Peterson, S. M., Peterson, L. D., & Lacy, L. N. (2003). *How to deal with students who challenge and defy authority.* Austin, TX: PRO-ED.

Sheridan, S. M. (1995). *The tough kid social skills book.* Longmont, CO: Sopris West.

KEY WORDS

COOPERATIVE PLAY: When two or more children are working together toward one goal

PLAY: To take part in an enjoyable activity that creates an opportunity for teaching moments

SOCIAL SKILLS: Proper skills that are valued by society

TURN TAKING: A chance for children to learn all types of social skills just by interacting with one another through an activity

SEE ALSO THESE RELATED ENTRIES:

DEVELOPING SOCIAL SKILLS IN YOUNG CHILDREN WITH AUTISM

Judith Terpstra

SOCIAL SKILLS

Social skills are things that we all do during our daily activities that help us to get along with other people. For adults, social skills may include answering the phone appropriately, knowing when it is time to leave a friend's house or end a conversation, and knowing how to ask for help or how to act during a party or business meeting. For young children, social skills are things like sharing toys, asking to join a group or activity, initiating or responding during a social interaction, and asking a question or asking for help. Social skills also can include saying "Please" and "Thank you," dealing with feelings and stress, and making friends.

SOCIAL SKILLS AND CHILDREN WITH AUTISM

Young children with autism often lack the essential social skills that many children without disabilities have developed naturally.

Children with autism can still learn these skills, but they need to be taught in a predictable and systematic way. Skill deficits may appear in two ways. One is that the child may not know what to do in a certain situation and may just need to be taught. The other is that the child may know what is appropriate in a certain situation but not be able to perform the skill due to anxiety, fear of the situation, or for an unknown reason. Teaching social skills involves offering good models, breaking the steps down into sequences, and using a reinforcement system to encourage the child to practice and learn the skill.

SUGGESTIONS FOR TEACHING SOCIAL SKILLS

One way to teach play skills to children with autism is through a formal social skills training program. Many programs can be found on the Internet or at some bookstores. Some of these programs select certain social skills (e.g., sharing, asking for help, commenting, joining in a group) and break them down into smaller steps that can be taught easily to children. Other types of programs have a short-term strategy to teach the child with autism to remember what to do in certain situations. No matter what program is used, children must have plenty of opportunities to practice the skills with other children in a safe place where praise and correction can be given when needed by a parent or teacher. The following sections offer strategies to follow to teach social skills.

FIND OUT WHICH SOCIAL SKILLS AREAS YOUR CHILD NEEDS

1. Watch your child in situations with other children and adults.

2. Ask teachers and other school staff to keep a log or checklist of your child's social skills.
3. Ask other children that your child interacts with during the week to discuss what makes a good friend and why other children want or do not want to play with your child.
4. Determine if the skill is something your child has not learned yet or if your child knows it but does not do it or does not do it correctly.

DECIDE ON AN INTERVENTION STRATEGY

1. Work with your child's teachers to develop a strategy.
2. Use a strategy from a book or Web site.

IMPLEMENT THE INTERVENTION

1. Be consistent.
2. Provide reinforcement praise for use of the skill.
3. Provide many good examples of the skill being used every day.
4. Provide many opportunities for your child to practice using the skill every day.

ASSESS AND MODIFY
THE INTERVENTION AS NECESSARY

1. Adapt the intervention as needed and avoid creating a frustrating situation for you and your child.
2. Remember that no one program will work for every child and every family. You know your child's needs and when an intervention needs to change.
3. Ask for help: Talk to other parents, teachers, support groups, and professionals.

USING SOCIAL SKILLS IN NATURAL SETTINGS

Children with autism need opportunities to play with other children. The children with autism can practice their social skills and also see models of how other children use skills in the same situation. Play groups or classes with cooperative, friendly children without disabilities that are structured so that the nondisabled children know what skills the child with autism is working on also can be helpful. Nondisabled children can help give reminders, provide reinforcement, and redirect children with autism if they understand their role in the situation.

PRINT RESOURCES

Guill, K. A. (2000). *Do-watch-listen-say: Social and communication intervention for children with autism*. Baltimore: Brookes.

Knoff, H. M. (2002). *The stop & think social skills program*. Longmont, CO: Sopris West.

McGinnis, E., & Goldstein, A. P. (1990). *Skillstreaming in early childhood*. Champaign, IL: Research Press.

KEY TERMS

PLAY SKILLS: Behaviors associated with appropriate or cooperative play

SOCIAL SKILLS: Behaviors associated with appropriate initiation, responding, or interaction with others

SEE ALSO THESE RELATED ENTRIES:

FUNCTIONAL LIVING SKILLS

STRATEGIES FOR TEACHING DAILY LIVING SKILLS

E. Amanda Boutot

FOR many of us, learning to brush our teeth, get dressed, make ourselves something to eat, or take care of our belongings comes naturally. For children with autism, this is not always the case. These children often need specific instruction in learning skills, called *daily living skills,* because otherwise they might not learn them at all. Children with autism all learn differently, and each child has different needs that are uniquely his or hers. This entry describes various examples of daily living skills, ways to determine which ones your child with autism may need specialized instruction to learn, and some strategies that you can use to help teach these to your child.

WHAT ARE DAILY LIVING SKILLS?

Daily living skills encompass anything that we would consider a normal part of one's day, such as eating meals, cleaning up, and getting ready for bed. Although most children acquire these skills at various stages based on maturity and age, children with autism may take longer to show an interest in or ability to do them. Many children with autism become easily accustomed to routines; therefore, if they have grown used to a caregiver always dressing them, for example, they are unlikely to want to do this activity on their own. You as a parent can aid in moving your child with autism closer to independence by occasionally permitting him or her to attempt tasks on his or her own. One example would be to have your child attempt to pull up his or her pants or pull on his or her shirt. You might start with the clothing item halfway on and encourage your child to finish the task. Some children will have seen their parents do this so many times that they naturally will reach down (or up) and finish putting the item on; others will require more specific instruction to learn to do the skill.

HOW DO I KNOW WHEN MY CHILD IS READY TO LEARN?

Watch for clues that your child is ready and able to care for his or her own daily living needs. Watch what other children the same age as your child are able to do for themselves, and then test your child to see if he or she might be able to do similar tasks. For example, put the cereal bowl and cereal on the table but wait to see if he or she will try to pour the cereal into the bowl. Although many children with autism may not immediately begin a task, you can determine how ready your child is by seeing how long it takes him or her to show an interest in it. If after several seconds or minutes, your child still has shown no interest, it may be wise to wait until he or she is a bit older before attempting to teach that skill. One of the most crucial components to the success of any teaching strategy is the child's motivation; without it, learning will come much more slowly and will take much more work.

WHAT AREAS SHOULD I START TEACHING?

Teaching daily living skills is best accomplished in the natural environment with natural materials. In other words, it is not wise to try to teach brushing hair by having a child pretend to brush a doll's hair; he or she should be taught with a real brush, in front of a mirror, and on his or her own hair. As noted before, it is best to watch your child to see what skills he or she might be interested in and able to learn. Success in one area will lead to greater independence, which will lead to more motivation to learn skills in other areas. If your child is motivated by food, you might want to start with eating skills, such as feeding, making simple snacks, and cleaning up.

FORWARD CHAINING

One example of a strategy you might use is *forward chaining*, where you teach your child one small subskill of a larger skill at a time, starting with the first and progressing through to the last. This is wise when the skill is particularly difficult or new to your child. Breaking down skills (such as brushing the teeth) into smaller subskills is called *task analysis*. For example, brushing teeth is a larger skill that involves many subskills, such as turning on the water, wetting the brush, removing the cap from the toothpaste, squeezing paste onto the brush, brushing, rinsing the brush, rinsing the mouth, and turning off the water. The level of detail should match the abilities of your child. Trying to teach the entirety of brushing teeth all at once may be overwhelming, but when it is broken down into smaller steps, it is more manageable and easier to learn.

PICTURE CUES

Create pictures as cues to the different steps in the process. This can be done for any task, and pictures can be found in magazines, cut out from published materials (e.g., Boardmaker), or taken with a camera. Display the pictures from top to bottom, in order from the first step to the last one in the sequence, and place them in a location that is easily seen while performing the task (e.g., on the bathroom mirror for brushing teeth or washing hands). You can refer to the pictures as you guide your child through the steps.

BACKWARD CHAINING

A second strategy that often is successful in teaching daily living skills is called *backward chaining* and involves teaching sub-skills in the reverse order. For example, when teaching how to make a sandwich, you might start with putting the two pieces of bread together after all ingredients are on them, followed by teaching placing ingredients, followed by getting ingredients from the cupboard, and so forth. Children who are not terribly motivated by the task will see its conclusion more quickly and become more motivated to learn the skills for completing the task. Another example of backward chaining often is used when teaching children how to get dressed or undressed. Start with the shirt almost completely off, such as up to the top of the head, and then ask your child to finish pulling it off, progressing to the point where he or she grasps it from the bottom and lifts it over his or her head.

SUMMARY

When using either form of chaining, your child does not have to be able to do each subskill perfectly before you move on to the next skill. Just be sure that he or she is able to complete at least some portion of each skill on her or his own before you move on to a new skill to avoid frustration. Often moving from one skill to another is motivating and helps children see the value of each skill as it relates to the others. Above all, use a lot of praise for accomplishment, as well as attempts, and avoid negative comments when your child is not successful. Remember, the key to success is motivation.

PRINT RESOURCE

Scheuermann, B., & Webber, J. (2002). *Autism: Teaching does make a difference*. Belmont, CA: Wadsworth.

KEY TERMS

CHAINING: Strategy for teaching a new skill by teaching small component parts of the skill separately and adding subsequent parts until the whole skill can be performed independently

PICTURE CUES: Symbols used to provide structure or serve as a reminder of the steps to follow in a task

SEE ALSO THIS RELATED ENTRY:

4.3   Picture-Based Communication Systems . . . . .p. 111

USING PROMPTS TO HELP YOUR CHILD LEARN

Jennifer Migliorini, Tabitha J. Kirby, and Stephanie M. Peterson

CHILDREN with autism often need a little extra help to learn desired skills. Prompts are tools that you can use to help your child be successful and learn efficiently. This entry describes what prompts are, when they should be used, and how to use them most effectively.

WHAT IS A PROMPT?

Prompts are supplementary cues you can use to increase the likelihood that your child will respond correctly in the presence of a natural cue. In other words, a prompt is some sort of extra assistance you provide to help your child perform the desired skill. The purpose of a prompt is to allow your child to succeed at a skill that is being taught or reviewed.

VERBAL PROMPTS

Verbal prompts are when you tell your child what he or she should do in response to an instruction or event. For example, in teaching a child to answer the telephone, you might use the verbal prompt, "Pick up the phone and say, 'Hello.'"

GESTURES AND MODELS

Gestures and models are prompts that can help show your child how to perform the behavior. *Gestures* often are used when your child knows what to do but needs assistance in getting started on the task. For instance, if your child is helping set the table and is holding a spoon in his or her hand, you might point to the right side of the knife already on the table to show where the spoon should go. Gesture prompts take the place of more intrusive physical prompts.

Modeling actually is demonstrating the behavior for your child to imitate. For example, when setting the table, you might actually take a spoon and set it in its proper place to show your child how to set the table. Your child would then repeat the behavior.

PHYSICAL PROMPTS

Physical prompts involve you physically helping your child perform the desired behavior. Physical prompts can be either full or partial. A *full physical prompt* is when you place your hand or hands directly over your child's hands and direct him or her through the task. This prompt might be used during very difficult tasks or when your child does not respond when given a verbal prompt or a model prompt. A *partial physical prompt* is when you do part of a task with your child but then allow him or her to complete the rest of the skill. For example, if you were prompting your child to take off her or his pajama top using partial physical prompts, you might help your child put her or his hands on the bottom part of the top and then help to begin pulling the top over his or her head. You might remove your physical assistance at that point and allow your child to pull the top over his or her head alone.

STIMULUS PROMPTS

Stimulus prompts are different from response prompts because they do not involve adding additional cues to the natural cues. Instead, stimulus prompts involve altering the natural cues in some way to make them more effective. One form of stimulus prompting involves positioning the cue closer to your child to increase the likelihood that he or she will perform the correct behavior. For example, if you want your child to remember to put his or her pajama top in the clothes hamper after taking it off, you might place the clothes hamper next to the dresser (assuming your child stands in front of the dresser when getting dressed) rather than in the bathroom. Another kind of stimulus prompt involves making natural cues more noticeable. For example, if a teacher wants a child to remember to put her or his name on a paper, the teacher might bold or highlight the word *name*.

Enunciation prompts are another form of stimulus prompt used when working on articulation, question discrimination, and other concepts, such as counting. In this case, the adult enunciates key words in the instruction to help the child discriminate what is being asked. For example, when teaching a child how to respond to the questions, "How old are you?" and "How are you?" you might stress the word *old* when presenting the question to help the child hear the difference in the two sentences.

USING PROMPTS EFFECTIVELY

WHEN SHOULD PROMPTS BE GIVEN?

Prompting procedures often are needed when a behavior or skill is first being introduced and you know that your child does not know how to do it. Prompts should be considered part of the teaching process. They allow you to reinforce your child for the desired behavior even though he or she cannot yet perform the behavior independently. As your child learns the behavior, he or she will be reinforced without the prompts. In addition, prompts also can be used after the behavior has been learned if your child begins to make errors, performs the behavior incorrectly, or loses motivation to perform the behavior.

To be most effective, prompts should be delivered as soon as possible following the natural cue. This allows your child to perform the behavior as quickly as possible, so that he or she will begin to associate the natural cue with the desired behavior rather than with the prompt.

HOW DO I KNOW WHICH PROMPT TO DELIVER?

In general, if you are teaching a new skill you may want to begin with more intrusive prompts to ensure that your child is success-ful. If your child already can do part of the skill, you may be able to begin with a less intrusive prompt.

HOW CAN I AVOID HAVING MY CHILD BECOME TOO DEPENDENT ON PROMPTS?

This is a very valid concern. If you are not careful, your child may begin to rely on your prompts rather than performing the behavior when the natural cues are present. To avoid this, you need to fade (lessen) your prompts as quickly as possible. First, always try to use the least intrusive prompt necessary to get the behavior to occur. As your child begins to display the correct behavior frequently, try to use a less intrusive prompt the next time the opportunity presents itself and see if your child displays the correct behavior. If he or she does not, you can use a more intrusive prompt, but at least you gave your child the opportunity to do the behavior with a less intrusive prompt first. For example, if you have just begun teaching your child to brush her or his teeth, you may choose to physically prompt your child through the task. As your child begins to do some of the steps a little more independently, you might begin using verbal prompts, such as, "What do you need to do next?" or "Put the toothpaste on." You could then slowly fade the verbal prompts until your child brushes his or her teeth independently.

Some people find a procedure called *time delay* to be useful in fading prompts. When using time delay, you wait a specified amount of time after the natural cue occurs before providing a prompt. For example, if you are teaching your child to pick up blocks after he or she is done playing, you might say, "Clean up the blocks," and then wait 2 seconds. If your child does not respond, you would then prompt him or her through the task of picking up the blocks. To fade your prompts, you can begin to increase this delay by waiting 4 seconds, then 6 seconds, then 10 seconds, and so on until your child no longer needs a prompt.

SHOULD I REWARD THE DESIRED BEHAVIOR EVEN THOUGH I HAD TO USE A PROMPT?

Yes! It is very important that you praise and reward your child for performing the desired behavior, even if you had to prompt for it. Remember, learning occurs in a three-step process (*antecedent, behavior, consequence*). Without a positive consequence following the desired behavior, your child probably will not learn to do the behavior when the natural antecedent cue is present.

SUMMARY

In this entry, you learned what prompts are, when they should be used, and how to use them effectively. Prompts are a key component when teaching children with an autism spectrum disorder. They provide the extra boost your child might need to be successful.

PRINT RESOURCE

Van Houten, R. (1998). *How to use prompts to initiate behavior.* Austin, TX: PRO-ED.

KEY TERMS

PROMPT: Some sort of extra assistance you provide to help your child perform a desired skill

PROMPT FADING: Increasing the time delay by units until your child no longer needs a prompt

RESPONSE PROMPTS: Verbal prompts, gestures/models, and physical prompts; involves adding additional cues to help your child respond correctly after the natural cue has occurred

STIMULUS PROMPTS: Altering the natural cues in some way to make them more effective

THREE-TERM CONTINGENCY: The concept that learning occurs through antecedent, behavior, and consequence

TIME DELAY: Waiting a specified amount of time after the natural cue occurs before providing a prompt

SEE ALSO THESE RELATED ENTRIES:

ISSUES IN TOILETING

E. Amanda Boutot

ALTHOUGH most children learn to use the bathroom independently between the ages of 2 and 3 years, children with autism often do not, perhaps due to language or cognitive deficits related to their autism. This does not mean, however, that toileting should not be a priority for these children. In the past, it was customary to try to teach toileting through long sessions on a toilet using liquids to stimulate production of urine. This no longer is an accepted practice. This entry presents some of the signs parents can look for that their child is ready to learn to toilet, as well as some steps for ensuring success.

SIGNS THAT YOUR CHILD MAY BE READY TO TOILET

First, children should be at least 2 ½ years old before you begin to consider toileting. Though some typically developing children may show an interest earlier, it is unusual for successful independence to occur much earlier than this age. Second, watch your child for signs that he or she has some control over the bowel and urinary tract muscles, usually if he or she is able to remain dry for a period of at least 1 to 2 hours. Finally, carefully watch the times of day that your child does wet or soil his or her diaper, looking for a pattern that indicates some predictability for instruction. When you see a pattern and your child has shown the ability to consistently "hold it" for longer periods of time, it may be time to start toileting instruction.

STEPS IN TOILETING INSTRUCTION

Although it may be difficult for today's busy families, the first and perhaps most important step to a successful toileting program is the collection of baseline data. This means keeping a careful log of the times of day that your child wets and soils his or her diaper. Again, you are looking for patterns. A chart often is recommended so that a clear pattern for preferred times of day could be determined. Second, start by taking your child to the toilet during the times of day that he or she typically wets or soils the diaper (as determined in the first step). Your child does not have to be successful while in the bathroom, but if he or she is, praise lavishly! During the second step, make all diaper changes, when possible, in the bathroom so that your child begins to associate the bathroom with all things related to urination and bowel movements. At first, the number of times that you take your child to the toilet each day may be more numerous than he or she actually needs to go; this will help to establish a pattern and will give him or her more of a chance to succeed once in there.

KEYS TO TOILETING SUCCESS

There are many reasons why your child may not begin toileting on his or her own, even with instruction. One is that he or she simply is not ready. Watching for readiness cues will help you select a time when your child is more likely to succeed. Another common reason is control. Children typically begin to have a desire to control more of their world at about ages 2 to 3, and again at puberty, and children with autism are no different. Many times, a young child or a child with a disability will find that there is very little that he or she actually can control, given limitations, adult involvement, and so forth. It is at these times that your child may discover his or her ability to "control" toileting habits. If you suspect that your child might be using toileting as a control mechanism (for example, holding urine or bowel movements all day or in certain situations), he or she may be indicating a need for control.

One method that has been effective in helping children who have difficulty with toileting to feel more control over their lives is to provide more choices in other areas. For example, offer a choice of things to eat at breakfast or snack or a choice of activities or places to go. The more control your child begins to feel, the more likely he or she may be to let go of some of the control in the toileting area. This is especially true if you consistently use the steps listed above.

The use of picture-cued schedules will help provide more control and help in toileting itself. Create pictures depicting what activities your child will be doing throughout the day and place them in sequential order somewhere in your house where he or she easily can see them. You can allow your child some choices over the activities by showing him or her two or three pictures and letting him or her choose which one to put on the schedule. As activities are finished, move them from the board to a "Finished" envelope or box (some location other than the schedule to indicate that they have been completed). Insert several pictures depicting toileting so that your child knows in advance that this will be happening throughout the day. The use of the pictures— and having them in a prominent, accessible place—should eventually lead to your child using the pictures to indicate his or her need to use the bathroom, even in times when it is not on the schedule. Always say where you are going and why as you lead your child to the bathroom, and begin to allow him or her to walk there on his or her own as soon as possible to further encourage independence.

No toileting program will be successful without consistency. All family members and potential caregivers must understand and know what to do. This includes teachers at your child's school. If you are using a schedule system, you should ask your child's teacher to use one as well. Also, encourage the school staff to follow a similar schedule for toileting, as well as similar procedures when in the bathroom. Many children with autism will have toileting goals or objectives on their Individual Education Programs (IEPs), and the IEP meeting is a good time to discuss the steps that may work best. Consistency between home and school will promote success more quickly than if the program is only done in one place. In addition, do not use a toileting schedule or program that your family may not be able to consistently follow: It is better to start slowly and build a strong program than to try to do too much and end up being inconsistent.

Finally, be sure to praise your child lavishly, perhaps even offering a reward, for each successful trip to the toilet. Remember to check the diaper periodically between bathroom visits and to offer praise for dryness. Do not punish or scold your child for dirty or wet diapers; this may only discourage your child and may cause him or her to see toileting as something negative. Toileting must be seen as a positive activity, as well as one that your child can do and control.

PRINT RESOURCES

Scheuermann, B., & Webber, J. (2002). *Autism: Teaching does make a difference*. Belmont, CA: Wadsworth.

Westling, D. L., & Fox, L. (2000). *Teaching students with severe disabilities* (2nd ed.). Upper Saddle River, NJ: Merrill/Prentice Hall.

KEY TERMS

BASELINE DATA: Records of how much time or how often a behavior occurs so that it can be compared to any changes that are the result of instruction

PICTURE-CUED SCHEDULES: Pictures depicting activities throughout the day to serve as a reminder and allow some choices

SEE ALSO THESE RELATED ENTRIES:

PROMOTING MAINTENANCE AND GENERALIZATION OF LEARNING

Michelle A. Anderson, Corinne M. Murphy,
Natalie J. Allen, Charles L. Wood,
Susan M. Silvestri, and William L. Heward

IF you are the parent of a child with autism, you may have noticed that your child sometimes has difficulties using a new skill in places that differ from the situations or settings in which he or she learned the skill. This is a problem with generalization, which often can be resolved with careful planning. This entry describes the different types of generalization and provides examples related to teaching the skill of responding to greetings.

WHAT ARE MAINTENANCE AND GENERALIZATION?

MAINTENANCE

Maintenance refers to your child's ability to continue performing a skill after instruction has stopped. Put another way, if your child maintains the skill, he or she remembers how and when to do it later. For example, Sam's mother taught him to say, "Hi," when his brother enters the house and says, "Hi, Sam." She taught him to do this by using verbal prompts ("Sam, say, 'hi'") and praise for correct responses. A month later, Sam continues to say, "Hi," to his brother when he enters the house even though his mother is no longer prompting or praising his efforts.

GENERALIZATION TO NEW SETTINGS OR SITUATIONS

This type of generalization exists when your child exhibits the skill in a new place, with new people, or in response to different events. This aspect of generalization is extremely important because skills rarely are useful if they can only be performed in one place, with one person, or in response to one specific cue or antecedent.

For example, after Sam was taught to greet his brother at home, he also says, "Hi," to his brother when he passes him in the hall at school (new place). Sam also greets his teachers and peers when they greet him (new people). Sometimes Sam's peers say, "Hey, Sam," or "Hello" (new antecedent) instead of "Hi." Sam is able to respond correctly by responding to all of these by saying, "Hi." Each of these examples represents generalization to a new situation.

RESPONSE GENERALIZATION

When your child performs the target skill in a new way, he or she is demonstrating response generalization. The behavior must still serve the same function (e.g., is still a greeting), but it looks or sounds different from the originally taught example. This type of generalization is an especially important consideration in language skills, so that your child's speech does not appear rote or scripted.

For example, when Sam's brother walks in the front door and says, "Hi," to Sam, Sam looks up and responds, "Hey there." This response is still an appropriate greeting for Sam to use but is different from "Hi," which is the response he was taught. Another example of response generalization would be for Sam to wave hello to his brother when he is greeted.

PLANNING FOR GENERALIZATION

Generalization is not the second phase of instruction; it should be planned and programmed from the beginning. It also is important to avoid the "train and hope" mentality. Although your child may occasionally show generalization of a skill without direct teaching, this result is less likely and is not reliable. The following section describes specific strategies that will increase the likelihood that a new skill will generalize.

INITIAL STEPS

Before deciding how to use these strategies with your child, you must create a plan for the skill you are teaching.

1. *Choose a target behavior.* When choosing a new skill to teach your child, begin with something that will be useful in your child's daily environment. For example, greetings are an important life skill for Sam to acquire. He is presented with many opportunities to greet people each day, and without this response he may be excluded from further social interactions. Once Sam initially learns to greet with the use of prompts and praise from his mother, he is likely to use natural reinforcers for this skill (e.g., smiles, continued social interaction).

TABLE 3
SAM'S GREETING BEHAVIOR

IMPORTANT SITUATIONS	RESPONSE VARIATIONS	RESPONSE CHARACTERISTICS

A. Places
  1. Home
  2. School
  3. Community
B. People
  1. Children
  2. Adults
C. Antecedents
  1. "Hi, Sam."
  2. "Hi."
  3. "Hello."
  4. "Hi there."
  5. Wave
	1. "Hi."
	2. "Hello."
	3. "Hi, (name)."
	4. "Hi there."
	5. Wave
	6. "What's up?"
		1. Look at person being spoken to
		2. Respond within 2 seconds of greeting
		3. Loud enough to be heard by person being greeted (except for hand wave)

2. *Make a list of important factors related to the target skill you have chosen.* List different settings, people, and events your child may interact with while using this new skill. Also, list different acceptable responses. Finally, think about how your child will need to be able to perform the skill for it to "work" in the natural environment. Table 3 is what such a list might look like for Sam's greeting behavior.

A PLAN FOR TEACHING

Now that you have chosen a skill to teach and listed important factors related to generalization, it is time to think about how you will increase the probability that the new skill will generalize. The following three strategies will help.

1. *Make the teaching setting similar to the natural setting.* Let's take a look at this step for Sam and his greetings. Sam is taught many skills during sessions with his teacher that take place at a table. This setting is appropriate for many skills but is

less relevant for greetings. Instead, Sam is taught greetings upstairs near the front door with his brother actually entering the house.

2. *Teach a variety of examples.* Examples that are taught during instruction should represent the range of situations your child will need to respond to or face in the natural environment. You should select teaching examples from the list you made during the planning stage. Doing this will increase the likelihood of directly teaching a situation similar to one your child will encounter in his or her daily life. For example, if Sam only responds with "Hi," he also may need to be directly taught response variations.

3. *Make sure the new skill gets reinforced.* When you are first teaching a skill, you probably will have to use contrived consequences (e.g., excited praise, access to tangible items, preferred treats) every time your child does the skill correctly. In the natural environment, however, consequences and reinforcement often are much more subtle and not as continuous. Beginning with continuous and heavy reinforcement will help your child learn the new skill. Once the skill is acquired, you should gradually reduce (fade) reinforcement until it is similar to the consequences in the natural environment.

When Sam's mother is first teaching him to respond to a greeting, she will be providing praise and toys every time Sam responds appropriately. As he becomes more successful, she will fade to randomly praising correct responses. Finally, she will completely fade her praise and allow Sam's brother's continued social interaction to function as a reinforcer.

HOW DO I KNOW WHEN GENERALIZATION HAS OCCURRED?

It is important to teach a skill until your child can use it in the natural environment. What should you do when you think your child has learned to use a skill satisfactorily?

PROBE

Arrange opportunities to observe your child in the setting the skill needs to be used in, or ask for reports from people who are in those environments. Sam's mother might ask his teacher if he has started responding to her greetings and the greetings of other teachers. She also might drive him to school one day so that she can watch to see if he greets other children. Taking a walk through the neighborhood or a trip to the playground would allow her to observe Sam's responses to various greetings from children and adults.

REVISE YOUR TEACHING

If the new skill you have been teaching has not generalized, or has only partially generalized, you can take some steps:

1. *Check to see if your child is performing the behavior well enough.* Sam may have said, "Hi," to other children, but he said it so quietly that they did not respond to him. When his mother checks in, it might look like he has not generalized the skill, but in fact it just did not receive reinforcement so he has stopped.
2. *If the generalization setting is too different from anything your child has seen, you should revise the teaching environment.* For example, Sam might need to have more specific instruction outside of his home to perform the skill at the playground or on a walk.

3. *There may be no reinforcement for the targeted behavior in the natural environment.* In this case, ask others to help. Sam's peers may not respond to him after he says, "Hi" (or may not even greet him in the first place) because for so long he did not know how to say, "Hi." In this case, Sam's mother can ask his teacher to teach the children how to respond.

CELEBRATE SUCCESS

If the new skill has generalized, it is time for you and your child to celebrate! Praise your child for his or her efforts and reward yourself for successful teaching. At this point, you can start the process for a new skill.

PRINT RESOURCES

Cooper, J. O., Heron, T. E., & Heward, W. L. (2005). *Applied behavior analysis* (2nd ed.). Upper Saddle River, NJ: Merrill/Prentice Hall.

Rosales, J., & Baer, D. M. (1998). *How to plan for generalization* (2nd ed.). Austin, TX: PRO-ED.

KEY TERMS

GENERALIZATION: The ability to perform a skill in settings or under different conditions from those in which the skill was taught

MAINTENANCE: The ability to perform a skill over time

REINFORCEMENT: Rewards for appropriate behavior or skills

SEE ALSO THESE RELATED ENTRIES:

USING NATURALISTIC INSTRUCTION FOR CHILDREN WITH AUTISM

E. Amanda Boutot

NATURALISTIC teaching is sometimes referred to as incidental teaching, which involves "teaching a child a particular skill in the context of its use" (Pierce & Schreibman, 1997, p. 288). Naturalistic teaching strategies involve several components: use of new materials, adults joining the activities with the children, choices, and use of incidental strategies (e.g., placing a preferred item out of reach so that the child must "ask" for it). Kohler, Anthony, Steighner, and Hoyson (2001) also noted that "using comments and questions to facilitate the child's interest and/or play-related talk," generating elaboration of child's talk, and inviting interaction with peers or siblings are components (p. 95). Naturalistic teaching strategies take advantage of teachable moments, as well as set up the environment so that those moments are most likely to happen. Naturalistic teaching strategies have been used to successfully teach play skills, social skills, appropriate behaviors, and communication skills to preschool children, as well as to children with autism. This entry will describe some typical naturalistic teaching strategies, as well as a common program (Floortime) that use these methods for children with autism.

TEACHABLE MOMENTS

First of all, teaching your child with autism does not have to occur at regularly scheduled times during a day or week. It can happen any place and at any time. By spending regular time with your child, you can find out what he or she enjoys or is interested in and take advantage of that interest to use in a teaching moment. For example, if your child especially is drawn to a specific book or video, sit with him or her when he or she is looking at it and ask questions such as, "Who is that?" or "What is the dog doing?" You are sharing your child's interest and also creating opportunities for communication. For a child who is nonverbal or for whom there is no communication system in place, setting up moments so that teaching can occur may be desirable. An example might be placing your child's favorite snack just out of reach but within eyesight. When he or she makes a motion or noise indicating that he or she wants the snack, you can prompt your child to use the communication system or speech as a way to get the snack. Once your child has successfully imitated you (or at least tried), give him or her the snack and praise. This is a common technique for teaching communication to very young children or those whose language is just emerging.

FLOORTIME

Described by Dr. Stanley Greenspan (Greenspan & Wieder, 1998), Floortime has been used successfully to incorporate play and social skills into the repertoire of children with autism. Floortime has several characteristics:

1. The adult follows the child's lead: Whatever the child finds interesting, the adult joins in.
2. The adult sits in front of the child so he or she becomes part of the child's world.
3. The adult joins the child's play: If the child repeatedly is rolling a car back and forth on a block, the adult does the same thing.
4. The adult is persistent. If the child pushes you away, do not leave but rather stay there and continue to be a part of his or her world.
5. The adult elaborates on play themes.
6. The adult uses a calm and encouraging voice and gestures.
7. The adult assists or models problem solving and creativity.

Though not typically used as a teaching session per se, Floortime can be a good opportunity to get into your child's world and help her or him expand the play he or she already does. It also might be appropriate to have older siblings join in Floortime, as long as they are able to participate without taking over. Eventually, you may model more appropriate play for your child who tends to use toys more for self-stimulation than for actual play. For example, you may model the extension of rolling the car on the block to rolling it on a track with sound effects. The goal is for play and social responding to become as typical as possible for your child through practice, modeling, and experience.

TIME DELAY

Once you have been doing some naturalistic teaching with your child for a while, you may find that he or she is learning a new skill. At this time, you may decrease your use of prompts or modeling and begin using what is known as a *time-delay procedure*: You ask a question or give a cue (e.g., put the snack out of reach) and wait a short time before offering any assistance to your child. Sometimes your child has a skill but needs a few seconds to produce it. Wait time is important because it encourages your child to be independent and prevents him or her from becoming too accustomed to help from adults.

SUMMARY

The purpose of naturalistic instruction is to provide a naturally occurring opportunity for your child to use or learn a skill so that generalization can occur more easily. Generalization is the concept of taking a skill learned in one setting or with one set of materials or instructions and being able to apply and use that skill elsewhere. Children with autism often have difficulty with generalization. Naturalistic instruction is a way to get around the need for specialized generalization training by teaching the skill in the context in which it typically will be used. The use of positive interactions—modeling and prompting only as necessary—and frequent positive feedback (positive reinforcement) make naturalistic instruction a powerful teaching tool. Natural environments are any in which your child chooses to spend time or that he or she typically is exposed to. Examples include a playroom, bathtub, a park, the grocery store, or preschool. Although it may be difficult at first, naturalistic instruction is best done with as little correction as possible but with continued support in the form of redirection (e.g., if necessary for safety), modeling, or limited prompting. Letting your child lead the way is the key to successfully learning the skill and being able to use it in other environments or under other circumstances. Especially in the case of Floortime, it also promotes appropriate social interactions with you and others by providing opportunities for your child to be near someone else in a positive, fun, and supportive way.

REFERENCES

Greenspan, S. I., & Wieder, S. (1998). *The child with special needs: Encouraging intellectual and emotional growth.* Reading, MA: Addison-Wesley.

Kohler, F. W., Anthony, L. J., Steighner, S. A., & Hoyson, M. (2001). Teaching social interaction skills in the integrated preschool: An examination of naturalistic tactics. *Topics in Early Childhood Special Education, 21,* 93–103, 113.

Pierce, K., & Schreibman, L. (1997). Increasing complex social behaviors in children with autism: Effects of peer-implemented pivotal response training. *Journal of Applied Behavior Analysis, 28,* 285–295.

WEB RESOURCES

Dr. Stanley Greenspan (http://www.stanleygreenspan.com)

Interdisciplinary Council on Developmental and Learning Disorders (http://www.icdl.com)

KEY TERMS

FLOORTIME: Program for engaging in respectful activities with your child designed to help him or her learn to elaborate and experience more of his or her world

GENERALIZATION: The ability to transfer or use skills in all settings independent of instruction

MODELING: Demonstration of a skill or activity

POSITIVE REINFORCEMENT: A desirable reward (e.g., praise or "high five") designed to increase the likelihood that a skill or behavior will be repeated in the future

PROMPTING: Offering assistance to a child when he or she needs it; may be in the form of a verbal suggestion (e.g., "Use both hands") or physical help (e.g., moving your child's hands together)

TIME DELAY: Providing a small amount of wait time between asking a question or providing an opportunity before offering a prompt or model; allows more independence for the child

SECTION 8

PROMOTING FRIENDSHIP AND INCLUSION

PREPARING YOUR CHILD FOR THE GENERAL EDUCATION CLASSROOM

Shannon Crozier

AN increasing number of children with autism are being educated in general education classrooms. Some of these children spend their entire day in this classroom, while others spend only part of the day there. If your child is going to be educated in a general education classroom for any part of the day, preparing him or her beforehand will make the transition more successful. Three steps to preparing your child are desensitizing, rehearsing, and using transition objects.

DESENSITIZATION

Children with an autism spectrum disorder (ASD) often get anxious and upset when things change. A new school or classroom represents a lot of change. The more anxiety your child tends to feel when changes occur, the earlier you want to begin preparing him or her, and the slower you want to proceed. Desensitizing is a process for becoming gradually accustomed to unfamiliar settings or events. The first step is to help your child become comfortable, or desensitized, to the new school and classroom.

Begin by driving by the school regularly and talking about it. Next, visit the playground so your child can get used to playing on the structures and in the field. If your child is very anxious and has difficulty going near the school, reward him or her for spending longer periods there while maintaining appropriate behavior. You might start with a 1-minute visit and work up from there.

Once your child is comfortable with the outside of the school, you can progress to visiting the inside. As with the playground, your child should set the pace for these visits. Perhaps he or she will be ready to see the whole school and his or her classroom on the first visit, or perhaps he or she will only be able to spend 1 minute in the front hall when it is quiet and empty. Either way, the goal is for your child to become comfortable with this new school. Visits usually can be arranged with the principal and new teacher. Sometimes your child's current teacher or staff can arrange visits as well. Some children will visit a new school two or three times. Others will visit once a week for several weeks. Decide with your child's educational team what will be most appropriate for your child.

REHEARSAL STRATEGIES

Rehearsal strategies allow your child to practice the transition before it occurs. The goal with all of these strategies is to repeat information about the new school so that it becomes very familiar. Some examples are social stories, calendars, picture books, and a schedule of the first day. A social story can be written about moving to a new school, the people in the new school, or what will happen there. These stories can be read frequently before school starts. See Entry 6.1 on social stories for more information on how to use and write them.

CALENDARS

Calendars are useful tools to help children understand time and how it is organized. Mark a wall calendar with the first day of school. You also can mark school visit days. At night, cross off the day with your child and count how many more days until the next visit and until school starts. Your child will be more prepared because he or she will be able to see when the change is happening.

PICTURE BOOKS

During your visits to the school, take photos of the building, playground, and any staff members your child will know. Make a book of the pictures with labels identifying them. Read this book frequently, talking about the people and places. Help your child learn the names of people and how to find those people when you visit the school.

VISUAL SCHEDULES

Establish a morning routine for school days. A visual schedule of the routine can go beside the calendar, on the fridge, or in your child's room. It should list all of the activities to be done on a school morning, such as getting dressed, brushing teeth, and eating breakfast. Adjust your child to the appropriate bedtime and rising time before the first day of school. If you can arrange a school visit one morning, you can practice the whole routine from rising to going inside the school. The more familiar the routines on the first day of school, the less anxiety and distress your child is likely to experience. See Entry 5.2 on schedule systems.

TRANSITION OBJECTS

A transition object is a preferred item that is used to distract or comfort your child during a difficult transition. A special new backpack or lunchbox could be appropriate choices for your child. Buy them before school starts. Use visuals or stories to teach your child that he or she gets this special item when it is time to go to school. When your child goes to the first day of school, reward him or her by giving this object to use.

SUMMARY

As a parent, you know your child best and will know what works well for him or her. The strategies in this entry are suggestions that have worked for other children, but each child is different. Some children need more transition support than others. The following resources provide more information for supporting behavior during transitions.

PRINT RESOURCES

Hodgdon, L. A. (1995). *Visual strategies for improving communication: Practical supports for home and school.* Troy, MI: QuirkRoberts.

Hodgdon, L. A. (1999). *Solving behavior problems in autism.* Troy, MI: QuirkRoberts.

McClannahan, L. E., & Krantz, P. J. (2003). *Activity schedules for children with autism.* London: Woodbine House.

KEY TERMS

DESENSITIZATION: A process of becoming gradually comfortable with events, people, and places that are frightening or upsetting

Rehearsal strategies: Practicing all or part of an activity before it happens

Transition object: Any object that provides a cue about the beginning of the transition or serves as a reminder of the next activity or reward

Visual schedule: A sequence of pictures or words outlining activities during a certain time

SEE ALSO THESE RELATED ENTRIES:

PREPARING THE GENERAL EDUCATION CLASSROOM FOR YOUR CHILD

Shannon Crozier

NCLUSIVE education—where a child with a disability partici-pates in the general education classroom—can be a rewarding but also stressful experience for you and your child. Whether your child is fully included in a general education classroom or spends only part of the day there, it will be a more positive expe-rience if everyone is prepared for what is to come. Preparing the general education classroom will differ, depending on whether your child is switching classrooms, coming from another local school, or moving from a school far away. For inclusion to be suc-cessful, everyone involved needs adequate training and support. Being positive and straightforward will help set everyone at ease and create an atmosphere of open communication.

EDUCATING CLASSROOM STAFF

General education classroom teachers typically have limited, if any, training in special education. The needs of children with disabilities can intimidate them, and they might worry that they lack the skills to give your child appropriate support. Before having a student with an autism spectrum disorder (ASD) in their classroom, teachers need opportunities to learn about the child and the disability. Check with your school district and ask what professional development opportunities are provided. Teachers should attend an Individualized Education Program (IEP) transition meeting to talk about your child's strengths, needs, and services. If possible, the new teacher should visit the previous classroom to observe your child in his or her familiar environment. Useful information for new classroom staff could include a copy of the current IEP, a list of preferred school activities, and a communication dictionary.

RESOURCES

A general education classroom may not include some of the resources that your child had in his or her previous classroom, such as certain books, toys, or manipulatives. All of the materials indicated on your child's IEP need to be available in his or her new classroom. If this includes specialized equipment for therapies, talk to the IEP team before school starts and ask if all of the items—including your child's preferred activities—are there. For example, if your child enjoys using puzzles during free time, it might be a good idea to ask if there are puzzles in the new classroom.

COMMUNICATION

Communication among the education team members is critical to successful inclusion. School staff members need time to meet and plan together. They also need time for home-school communication. At the beginning of the school year, set up a home-school communication system, for example, a daily checklist, a weekly phone call, or a monthly meeting. A structured routine for communication will help resolve many small issues.

EDUCATING OTHER CHILDREN

One of the benefits of inclusive education is the opportunity for friendships between children with and without disabilities. Although the behavior of a child with an ASD can be confusing to other children, they can learn to be friends. Peers need to understand ASD and learn the skills necessary to interact successfully with your child. How much should be taught and who should teach it are team decisions. It is important to protect the dignity and privacy of your child and your family while still opening the door for understanding. In general, other children need just enough information to understand and not to be confused or scared by unusual behavior. The classroom teacher, last year's teacher, a special education teacher, a family member, or a neighborhood friend could lead a class discussion. The goal of peer education should be to share strengths and to help the children see your child as an interesting, competent member of the class who is similar in many ways to themselves. Some specific information might include how to use a communication system, how to ask your child to play, and how to react to inappropriate behavior. If the adults are calm and demonstrate understanding and confidence, your child's classmates will be more relaxed and receptive.

EDUCATING OTHER PARENTS

Educating other parents is a personal decision for your family. Some parents send home a letter explaining their child's strengths and needs and welcoming friendships with other families. Another way to educate other parents is through individual friendships; for example, arrange play dates with classmates at your house, a local park, or other location and invite the other child's parents to come along. This allows you to pick a day and an activity that will be successful and allows the other parent to learn about your child in an inviting environment.

EDUCATING YOUR CHILD

In addition to preparing the general education classroom for your child, your child also must be prepared. Starting in a new classroom or school is stressful for all children. Use simple strategies. For example, visit the classroom and get to know the school. Mark the first day of school on the calendar and count down the days. For more information and ideas, see Entry 8.1 on preparing your child for the general education classroom.

SUMMARY

The first day in an inclusive classroom can be exciting and nerve-wracking for everyone. Good preparation will help ease many of the challenges of settling into a new classroom experience. The first days can seem full of the unexpected, so keep the big picture of belonging and learning in mind.

PRINT RESOURCES

Gray, C. (2000). *The new social story book: Illustrated edition*. Arlington, TX: Future Horizons.

Lord, C., & McGee, J. P. (Eds.). (2001). *Educating children with autism*. Washington, DC: National Academy Press.

McClannahan, L. E., & Krantz, P. J. (2003). *Activity schedules for children with autism: Teaching independent behavior.* London: Woodbine House.

Quill, K. A. (1995). *Teaching children with autism: Strategies to enhance communication and socialization.* New York: Delmar.

KEY TERMS

COMMUNICATION SYSTEM: Any augmentative or alternative communication tool; includes picture exchange systems, topic boards, voice-output devices, or other electronic communication tools

INCLUSION: Educating children with disabilities in the general education classroom for a majority of the school day

SOCIAL STORY: A short, child-specific story that provides detailed and accurate information about a social situation

SEE ALSO THESE RELATED ENTRIES:

POSITIVE BEHAVIOR SUPPORTS: PROACTIVE STRATEGIES FOR CHANGE

Shannon Crozier

CHILDREN with autism can display some challenging behaviors that may make it difficult for them to participate in school, family, and community activities. When an inappropriate behavior does occur, you can react in many ways; however, the best time to intervene is before the behavior occurs. A proactive approach can prevent behaviors from happening in the first place. Positive behavior supports are proactive strategies that aim to improve a person's quality of life, increase positive behaviors, and decrease problem behaviors. Positive behavior supports consist of two groups of interventions: those that change the child's behaviors and those that change the child's environment. This entry will discuss strategies for changing the environment. See Entry 5.5 for strategies to change behavior.

Behavior is a type of communication. Children with an autism spectrum disorder (ASD) often use their behavior to communicate their needs when they have no other way to do so. Changing the environment allows you to create a functional space that makes it easier for your child to communicate and meet his or her needs without using inappropriate behavior. Your expectations of your child do not change.

ENVIRONMENTAL REORGANIZATION

Children with an ASD often have difficulty organizing information in their minds and may become anxious when they are not able to understand or predict what is happening. By setting a routine and organizing the environment in a highly structured, predictable manner, you can reduce anxiety.

ROUTINES

Routines can be made for any activity—from getting dressed in the morning, to eating lunch, to going to the store. Visual supports for routines are very helpful (see Entry 5.2 for tips on using calendars and schedules). Using pictures or words, you can create a simple checklist of steps for each activity. This helps your child organize his or her thinking and behavior. The activity is now easier to understand and complete.

PHYSICAL ARRANGEMENT

The physical arrangement of the environment also can provide routine and structure. The more external the structure, the less your child has to rely on his or her internal understanding. Color coding and labels are two methods for organizing space and materials. An example would be using plastic bins to store your child's toys. On the outside of each bin, put a label with the word or a picture of the toys inside. A clearly organized, labeled environment is easy for your child to understand.

STIMULI

It also is important to think about other aspects of the environment. If your child is distracted by sounds at school, a table close to the door or the fan is a poor choice. If crowds are bothersome, perhaps your child can walk in the hallways before or after the other students.

BEHAVIORAL MOMENTUM

Behavioral momentum is a strategy for increasing behavioral compliance by changing how a request is made. All children prefer some activities to others. Asking your child to stop a preferred activity to do a nonpreferred activity often is a struggle, whether the child has or does not have an ASD. Behavioral momentum gets your child moving with other preferred activities before making the target request. For example, your child is watching a video and it is time to turn it off. First you get his or her attention and then say, "Touch your nose!" followed by "Give me hug!" and then "Time to turn off the video." Your child is already complying with small, pleasant requests and is more ready to comply with your target request. Sometimes one extra request might be enough. At other times, several requests may be required.

CHANGE THE BEHAVIOR OF SIGNIFICANT OTHERS

The behavior of other people has a significant impact on your child's behavior. By changing the way people interact with your child, problem behavior can be decreased. Everyone who works and plays with your child should know what he or she can tolerate and what is challenging for him or her. If, for example, your child is hypersensitive to light touch and has tantrums as a result, family and staff members should know how to use firm pressure to avoid causing an outburst.

VISUAL SUPPORTS

Visual supports are excellent tools for providing structure, organizing the environment, and supporting the behavior of others. Visuals can be made with words, pictures, or both. They can be used for anything from checklists, routines, and schedules to materials, rules, and communication books. Some examples of visuals already have been given. Posting a few key visuals on the refrigerator, for example, allows your child to ask for a drink instead of crying. A rule card for the car reminds her or him to keep the seatbelt on, use a quiet voice, and look out the window. Visual supports provide consistency for everyone (see Entries 4.2 and 5.2).

CHOICE

Choice is powerful. Children with disabilities often do not get to make many choices, and problem behavior may be the result of rarely being allowed to make their own decisions. You can offer your child safe, controlled choices. Allowing your child to choose the puzzle or video, the park to visit, or the vegetable for dinner are some examples. Even if there is not a choice of activities or items, you can provide choice as to timing or the order of events. Choosing to put on the pants or shirt first, brushing the child's teeth or washing his or her hands first, and turning off the computer now or in 5 minutes all are examples of offering some choices when the end result will be the same, no matter what comes first. See Entry 5.12.

SUMMARY

Positive behavior supports offer extensive opportunities to integrate strategies into daily activities. There are many ways to use them creatively and to make them fit your child's needs and your lifestyle.

PRINT RESOURCES

Hodgdon, L. A. (1995). *Visual strategies for improving communication: Practical supports for home and school.* Troy, MI: QuirkRoberts.

Hodgdon, L. A. (1999). *Solving behavior problems in autism: Improving communication with visual strategies.* Troy, MI: QuirkRoberts.

McClannahan, L. E., & Krantz, P. J. (2003). *Activity schedules for children with autism: Teaching independent behavior.* London: Woodbine House.

KEY TERMS

BEHAVIORAL MOMENTUM: Increasing a child's compliance by starting with small, simple, and pleasurable requests (e.g., "Give me a hug") before making larger demands

CHOICE: Allowing a child to select from two or more options

VISUAL SUPPORTS: Photos, drawings, written words, or any combination of these to provide concrete structure for communication

SEE ALSO THESE RELATED ENTRIES:

TRANSITION

SECTION
9

TRANSITION SERVICES FOR CHILDREN WITH AUTISM

Jennifer Boeddeker

AN autism spectrum disorder (ASD) is a developmental disability that results in an individual's difficulty in building communication skills along with social and emotional attachments. Historically, these impairments—coupled with a limited understanding of the capabilities of children with an ASD—offered little opportunity for independent living. Recently, more children with an ASD have been leaving the educational setting with skills that better equip them for independent living and employment. Better transition planning and developmental programs can result in more positive life outcomes for children with an ASD. Social and emotional skill development, along with vocational skills training, prepares children with autism to be functional, integrated community members.

WHAT IS TRANSITION?

Transition involves preparing and moving your child to the next level in his or her educational, emotional, and social development. Transitions occur at all levels of the educational process:

educational development, environment changes, and the life beyond the classroom. Transitions between stages require the school, the classroom teacher, your child, and you to work as a team to prepare for the demands of each new environment. Successful transition services and planning are evident when your child becomes more independent and requires less support after each transition.

WHO IS ELIGIBLE FOR TRANSITION SERVICES?

The Individuals with Disabilities Education Act (IDEA; 1990) states that *all* children with disabilities must receive transitional services to prepare them for life within and beyond the classroom. Specifically, Sections 300.132 and 300.29 state that services will be provided to promote smooth transitions across educational areas. Section 300.132 identifies transition from preeducational programs into preschool and kindergarten as a process of meetings and preparation procedures for the child prior to entering school. Section 300.29 states that high school transition services will be provided to promote movement from school to postschool activities. These transition programs may include vocational training, integrated employment (including supported employment), adult services, independent living, and community participation.

WHEN SHOULD TRANSITION PLANNING AND SERVICES BEGIN?

Transitional services should be provided at each educational level. They should begin during your child's preschool program all the way up to and including his or her posteducational life planning. Every effort needs to be made to ensure smooth transitioning across grade levels. Your child with an ASD can be sensitive to change and loss of routine, so both you and the school must begin preparing early. IDEA mandates that postsecondary transition planning begin no later than when the child is 14 years old. During an Individualized Education Program (IEP) meeting, you and your child, along with the school team, should develop a plan or "statement of transition service needs" that addresses her or his interests. This plan should be updated yearly until your child turns 16. The school must then begin using a transition program directed toward independent living and employment for your child.

WHAT CAN BE EXPECTED FROM THE SCHOOL IN PREPARING A STUDENT FOR TRANSITION?

The school should take the interests of both you and your student into consideration in preparing for transition. Remember, each person is an important participant in the transition planning and implementation process. The school staff, classroom teacher, your child, and you are a team that discusses and builds his or her future social, vocational, and educational needs. Your child's strengths and challenges, likes and dislikes, and levels of comfort and anxiety in public and social settings should help to direct future living and working experiences. Your child's teacher, using information shared and discussed about your child's interests and educational strengths, becomes vital in designing and ensuring vocational development for transition. The teacher will implement a curriculum to prepare your child for employment and independent living by providing job training opportunities and social-emotional skills development.

HOW CAN I PARTICIPATE IN TRANSITION PLANNING?

Be an advocate for your child with an ASD. No one knows her or his needs better than you, the parent; therefore, you must speak on behalf of your child. Encourage transition planning and development to be a school and community program that focuses on her or his best interests. Attend all meetings, especially IEP meetings that discuss your child's academic and social progress. Monitor dates and times of critical special events, such as reevaluation and annual meetings. Stay in contact with the teacher. Maintain an open, free line of communication between yourself and the teacher where you can share your thoughts, ideas, and concerns. Ask for a list of resources for adult services in your area, and contact these early in the planning process to help your child once he or she leaves school. Invite people from outside agencies to the IEP meeting in which transition will be discussed. Most importantly, help your child build *self-determination* by encouraging him or her to participate in transition planning. This is a vital step for your child to become more independent and comfortable with his or her future.

REFERENCE

Individuals With Disabilities Education Act, 20 U.S.C. §1401 et seq. (1990).

PRINT RESOURCES

Howlin, P. (1997). *Autism: Preparing for adulthood*. New York: Routledge.

Smith, M. D., Belch, R., & Juhrs, P. (1995). *A guide to successful employment for individuals with autism*. Baltimore: Brookes.

Welman, P. (1996). *Life beyond the classroom: Transition strategies for young people with disabilities.* Baltimore: Brookes.

KEY TERMS

LIFE SKILLS: Age-appropriate, functional, day-to-day skills required for independence (e.g., dressing, toileting, riding a bus, shopping, cooking, banking); also called daily living skills

PRE-EDUCATIONAL PROGRAMS: Early intervention services that are directed toward meeting a child's physical, cognitive, communicative, social, and emotional needs, such as family training, occupational and physical therapies, and early assessment services

SELF-DETERMINATION: The capacity to know yourself well enough to choose the things that may be good or bad for a given situation; includes problem-solving skills, decision-making skills, and self-awareness

SOCIAL SKILLS: Verbal (when able) and nonverbal communication in social settings; controlling aberrant behavior; learning social cues

SUPPORTED EMPLOYMENT: An employment service that focuses on helping a person successfully participate in an integrated work setting with his or her peers

VOCATIONAL SKILLS: Job-training tasks specific to the interests and abilities of a child, such as bussing tables for restaurants and stocking or packing at grocery stores

SEE ALSO THESE RELATED ENTRIES:

ESTATE PLANNING AND CARING FOR YOUR ADULT CHILD WITH AUTISM

E. Amanda Boutot and Corie Craig

ALL parents have hopes and dreams for their child's future. For parents of children with autism and Asperger's syndrome, these hopes and dreams often are infused with very real concerns and fears—concerns about how independent the child will be and whether he or she will have a job; fears that someone may take advantage of him or her or not take good care of him or her; and concerns about what will happen to him or her when they can no longer take care of their child. This entry, based on conversations with Corie Craig, mother of a 17-year-old boy with autism, will show how her family has found ways to prepare for their son's adulthood both in the very near future and when she and her husband are no longer around.

PLANNING FOR THE FUTURE

The Craig family began thinking about their son Kyle's future when he was very young. Most people agree that the sooner families begin to think about what they hope for their son or daughter as adults, the easier it will be to make these dreams a reality. The Craigs have worked with school personnel to create meaningful Individualized Education Programs (IEPs) for Kyle that focus on functional goals and independence. The Craigs have continued to be an integral part of the IEP team meetings, often voicing concerns where others may have feared stepping on toes. What they have looked for most were caring and compassionate teachers and staff so that the best interests of Kyle would always be at the forefront of everyone's mind in working with him. They have not, however, gone as far as to press a lawsuit against the school district, or even to threaten one. Says Corie, "I want the people who work with Kyle to do so because they want to, not because they are being forced to." This sentiment has strengthened her relationship with school district personnel and given her avenues that many parents may not have had. Corie says that she really hasn't done anything all that remarkable, but she has asked for things that she felt Kyle needed and has not been afraid to go to the "right" people to make things happen. Knowing who the right people are can be difficult to determine. The best strategy in planning for your child's future, whether it is the next school year's educational goals or what you hope he or she will be doing as an adult, is to keep an open mind while making clear what is important to your family and what you think is best for your child.

ESTATE PLANNING

Corie noted that it is her family's expectation that once Kyle graduates from school, he will work in some sort of community-based supported employment. She said:

> Once he's out of school, we don't feel that it's in his best interest to live as an adult in our home. He wants and needs indepen-

dence, just like anyone else. Kyle could live in a group home or in some sort of assisted-living facility. We're not totally happy with the options that sort of living arrangement provides, however, and we're considering other options. Rather than living in an existing group home, we're considering setting up his own group home for him. What we have in mind is to buy a home with Kyle (his name will be on the title along with ours). There is a special mortgage product available for this type of arrangement. The mortgage even has special flexibilities, including allowing the roommate or boarder income to be used in qualifying for the mortgage. Kyle can have a couple of his coworkers/friends become roommates in his home. They can jointly hire a caregiver, using their benefits through the new state fiscal intermediary program. By setting up his housing this way, we're providing Kyle with more control over his life. For example, if he doesn't get along with his caregiver, instead of having to move out of his home (which is the case in existing group homes), Kyle could simply replace his caregiver. This is less disruptive and gives Kyle more control over his living arrangements.

To help make this lifestyle happen, our family has been setting up a financial plan. To do this, we hired a company that specializes in estate planning for families with special needs. They can project how much financial help Kyle will need over his lifetime and map out a financial plan that will help make an independent life for Kyle possible. This was a tough decision at first, since such a plan is done on a fee basis. It was hard making the decision to actually write that check. But we're finding that if done properly, such a plan can actually pay for itself over time.

OTHER OPTIONS

Obviously, not all families have the resources to create the sort of living opportunity that the Craigs hope to have for Kyle. However, families may find that their son or daughter could benefit from some of the ideas Corie has shared, such as setting up a retirement program or savings plan specifically for your child with a disability, and creating a plan that clearly spells out who is responsible for the money and how it is to be used. Many parents have a will in place, but creating a financial future for your child with a disability may require a bit more planning and documentation. If a reasonably priced attorney in your area cannot be found, you might contact a nearby law school, as they often have services available to the public free of charge or at very low rates. There also are parent organizations that may be able to help families create their own plan through inexpensive or minimal legal assistance.

Above all, planning is key to the success your child will have as an adult, and it cannot start early enough. As Corie mentioned, to help Kyle have the greatest amount of independence as an adult, what they plan for him now is of paramount importance. She said, "Unlike previous generations, our child with special needs will most likely outlive us, creating the need for us to provide for the lifestyle that we want him to have."

WEB RESOURCES

Ability First (http://www.abilityfirst.org)

Life Trust Planning (http://www.life-trust.com)

Med Support FSF International (http://www.medsupport.org)

United Cerebral Palsy of Middle Tennessee: Retirement and Estate Planning Tools (http://ucpnashville.org/estateplan.html)

KEY TERMS

INDIVIDUALIZED EDUCATION PROGRAM: A plan developed by a team of individuals who are "stakeholders" in the child's education; reviewed annually and includes a statement of the child's current abilities; a statement of needs; and specifics as to what will be taught, by whom, and how often it will be evaluated

LIFE SKILLS: Age-appropriate, functional, day-to-day skills required for independence (e.g., dressing, toileting, riding a bus, shopping, cooking, banking); also called daily living skills

SEE ALSO THIS RELATED ENTRY:

9.1   Transition Services for Children With Autism . . . . . . p. 303

ABOUT THE EDITORS

E. Amanda Boutot, Ph.D., is a Board Certified Behavior Analyst and assistant professor of special education at Texas State University, where she is the coordinator of the graduate program in autism and applied behavior analysis. Dr. Boutot's research is in early identification and early intervention in autism.

Matt Tincani, Ph.D., is a Board Certified Behavior Analyst and associate professor of special education at Temple University, where he specializes in the learning needs of children with autism spectrum disorders, applied behavior analysis, and positive behavior support.

INDEX

by Entry

Fine motor and gross motor development: 1.1, 3.3, 5.10
Floortime: 7.5
Fragile X syndrome: 1.2
Free appropriate public education (FAPE): 1.3, 2.1
Functional analysis: 5.3, 5.9
Functional behavioral assessment (FBA): 5.3
Functional communication: Intro, 3.2

G
Generalization: 5.4, 5.8, 5.10, 7.4, 7.5
Gestures: 7.2

H
Hand-over-hand prompting: 5.2, 5.10
High-tech communication systems/devices: 4.2, 4.3, 4.5
Holophrase: 1.1
Home-based services: 3.1
Hyperlexia: 4.7

I
IEP team: 2.1, 2.2, 2.3
Imitation: 1.1, 1.2, 4.1, 5.10
Incidental teaching: Intro, 7.5
Inclusion: 8.2
Increasing appropriate behavior: 5.5, 5.12
Indirect assessment: 5.3
Individualized Education Program (IEP): 2.1, 2.2, 2.3, 3.4, 7.3, 8.2, 9.1, 9.2
Individualized Family Service Plan (IFSP): 3.4
Individuals with Disabilities Education Act (IDEA): 1.3, 2.1, 2.3, 3.4, 5.3, 9.1

Intervention: Intro, 1.1, 1.2, 1.4, 2.1, 3.1, 3.3, 3.4, 3.5, 4.6, 5.6, 5.9, 6.3, 8.3

J
Joint attention: Intro, 1.1

L
Least restrictive environment (LRE): 2.1
Life skills: 9.1, 9.2
Line drawings: 5.2
Low-tech communication systems/devices: 4.2, 4.3, 4.5

M
Maintenance: 5.4, 7.4
Modeling: 4.4, 5.10, 7.2, 7.5
Model prompt: 5.10, 7.2
Multicomponent behavior plan: 6.1

N
Natural consequences: 5.8
Naturalistic teaching/instruction: 4.1, 7.5
Nonverbal imitation: 5.10

O
Observational learning: 5.10
Occupational therapy: 3.3

P
Parent Teacher Association: 2.2
Parent–teacher conference: 2.2
Perspective sentence: 6.1
Pervasive developmental disorder–Not otherwise specified (PDD-NOS): 1.2, 1.3, 1.4, 4.2
Physical therapy: 3.3
Picture-based communication systems: 4.1, 4.3, 4.5
Picture books: 8.1
Picture cues: 5.1, 7.1